Nicole
I hope
and add
you think wow
know about it
looking
forward to our
conversation

# Clear Water

## Pam Rowe

Lots of
love
Pam xx

MARCIA M
PUBLISHING HOUSE

# Clear Water

Authored by Pam Rowe

©copyright Pam Rowe 2018

Edited by Marcia M Publishing House Editorial Team Published by Marcia M Spence of Marcia M Publishing House, Oldbury, West Midlands the UNITED KINGDOM B69

ISBN-13: 978-1999611323

ISBN-10: 1999611322

**MARCIA M**
PUBLISHING HOUSE

*www.marciampublishing.com*

# Dedications

I dedicate this book to my son. When I told him some of my story and my intention to write, he encouraged me and helped by writing the chapter headings. He was only a teenager then. Over the years, as I shared aspects of my story with him, he only ever saw the lessons, the strength and how I have helped him as a result. He has always been proud of me.

To my two nieces, thank you for encouraging me to write more of the story than I originally intended. I hope this helps our family.

I also dedicate this book to all my friends who, over the years, have told me their stories, some with aspects like mine. For all of us, our experiences have resulted in a determination to be better parents than our parents were.

# Acknowledgements

To the mother figures in my life and my biological mother, thanks for my experiences because of the understanding I gained as a result. To my father, I guess you did what you came to do on a number of levels, and you too contributed to what I now know and what I do with what I know.

# Endorsement

Pam Rowe has turned her own experiences into a framework which can help and inspire others to understand what children need. Pam's resilience in overcoming multiple childhood adversities is also an inspirational call to social work from a social worker who speaks with the benefit and authenticity of having been there herself. Pam continued into adulthood battling to overcome the consequences of her childhood and to give something back to future generations of vulnerable children.

**Anthony Douglas – Chief Executive -** Children and Family Court Advisory and Support Service. (Cafcass)

# Reader Review

"This is the story of an incredibly special child, who has achieved her dreams in spite of heart-breaking experiences caused by adults in her early life. Pam was able to do this when she had very few adults who believed and trusted her.

In her first book, *Clear Water*, Pam provides earnest insight to all adults in their interactions with children. The book is deeply captivating, sophisticated, challenging and incredibly moving. This is one of the most stimulating stories that leaves the reader with lots of emotions, question marks and deliberations about human beings and the value of childhood.

Pam reminds us all that the way we respond to children has a deeper meaning to them and impact on their development. With great dexterity and emphatic style, she supports and challenges our understanding of children's world, their behaviour and more importantly their need for love and compassion. By its tremendously compelling nature, *Clear Water*, encourages parents and caregivers to reflect more on their parenting, how they relate to their children and time they spend with them. It provokes readers to understand not only children's need for love and compassion but also the need to express these emotions physically.

I am deeply inspired by the book; I remember giving my children a hug and telling them how much I love them and how special they are. After reading about Pam's story, I told my children that they could achieve their dreams and I will be there for them."

**Dr Onder Beter, PhD –** Father and Leader of Services to Children.

# Clear Water

## Pam Rowe

# Prologue

*My journey to clarity...*

# Prologue

I have been to many places in my quest to write this book. They have included the strong compulsion to put my story down on paper, experiencing the pain as I relived the episodes and wanting to put it down and stop writing about what some would view as unspeakable.

I hope this book will achieve what I intended, which is, that at least one person finds value in it, for themselves and perhaps for their children or the children they care for.

The title is *'Clear Water'* because the writing process has added another layer of release from the cloudy, murky, stained effect of my past experiences on my self-perception.

I had a fear of judgement. Whose judgement? I thought it would be people's judgement, but as I wrote, I discovered that I had been judging myself.

Everyone has good and bad experiences. My bad experiences are the link and the catalyst for the contribution that I am making today and will continue to make in the future. I believe it was the route to my purpose to serve humanity, it was also the route to understanding my resilience.

Writing this book has been the achievement of a journey to clarity.

*"This book is for you. it is for children, it is for adults, it is simply just for human beings."*

**Pam Rowe, Clear Water (2018)**

# Early Days in Jamaica

My most abiding memory is the loud evening call of my name spelt out letter by letter, "P-A-M." This was how I was greeted every evening by Uncle John with his booming voice when he came home, parking his Morris Minor car at the gate.

"Yes, Uncle John," I answered as I ran to greet him, giddy with excitement.

Uncle John was always laughing, his deep voice vibrating in the air as he reached into his side pocket to reveal a special treat, which was usually a packet of animal-shaped sweet biscuits or some molasses taffy.

When we reached the house, he put his bag down on the veranda, and spelled out "S-O-A-P." and "W-A-T-E-R." Off I'd go to get the soap from inside the house to bring it to him as he walked over to the enamel basin of water on the bench under the mango tree.

There he washed and dried his face to freshen up from a hard day's work in the sun. He worked as the District Superintendent of the local parish council, in charge of building all the roads in St. Thomas, Jamaica.

I sat eating my treat beside him as he talked to his wife, my Aunt Dar. I always felt happy being with them. Afterwards, Uncle John and I walked hand-in-hand around the yard.

We visited the two green talking parrots in the cage hanging on a low branch of our thick-limbed mango tree at the front of the house.

One of the parrots liked to say, "Shut-up, shut-up!" over and over again. This made my Uncle John laugh. We then sat on the two swings that hung from a higher branch until dinner was ready. That was our daily ritual.

I knew he loved me and I truly loved my Uncle John. He was a powerhouse of a man, weighing in at around 130 kg, over six feet tall. He had a dark complexion and a shiny balding head of thin, wavy black hair.

Uncle John's wife, Aunt Dar, was always a busy woman. She didn't laugh like my Uncle John, and she wasn't as talkative as he. She was always preoccupied with responsibility and wasn't much fun to be around.

Aunt Dar, had a full head of white hair. It was this way since she was a teenager. She wore plaits around the house and then when she was going out, she loosened them, combed and contained her hair in a hairnet. For special occasions, she gave her white locks a blue rinse.

Around the area, people called her the upper-class-lady, mainly because of her light-brown skin and family heritage, as they owned Orange Park, a former coffee plantation. Interestingly these things and her social status gave our family a high level of respect in the community.

Aunt Dar was an educated woman, having studied dentistry, an exceptional achievement for anyone growing up in the early 1900s. The death of her parents meant she was unable to complete her studies before she got married to her first husband.

At five feet eight inches, she was taller than other women I'd seen. She walked with a sense of importance and self-assurance without being arrogant. It mattered to her that she could help and support local people.

Aunt Dar told me she couldn't have children, having lost two during childbirth. As a result, she was chosen as 'godmother' to many children so they could have a better life. She helped with dinner money, school books and uniforms.

For the older girls who were not academically able, she thought it was vital for them to learn how to cook, clean, wash clothes and sew. All things to enable them to manage in life and attract a future husband.

She was a stickler for children speaking 'proper' English. No Jamaican patois could be spoken in her presence.

Aunt Dar welcomed the three children her husband, Uncle John, fathered with another woman. This was an enduring source of pain for her, but her guilt for not being able to bring a child into this world meant she gave them everything she could and then some.

She used her network of influential people to get her 'adopted' children into the best schools and the best jobs and even protection from the law when necessary.

I was another child in the household but under different circumstances. I was her only blood relative. Aunt Dar was my father's aunt (my great-aunt) who took me in aged two. I was the 'baby' of all the children living there, left to be myself without anything interfering with my thoughts. Then one day all that changed.

# The Cakes

It was the first day of May, May Day. The local Methodist churchyard, a mile away from our home, was bustling with chatter and children's laughter.

Ladies were laying the cakes they had made out on tables decorated with their best tablecloths. Although the main reason was to raise money for the church fund, they were really competing to prove who was most cultured and refined. Being refined meant you were formally taught how to bake, you could afford the best oven and could generally replicate the behaviour of the English middle and upper classes, a hangover from Colonial times.

After helping their wives, the husbands hung back at the front of the churchyard, leaning on their cars, talking and laughing amongst themselves. The children were playing at the side of the church, where the maypole was standing.

Aunt Dar had prepared six large sponge cakes, all feather light and moist, evenly golden, and perfectly shaped. Aunt Dar stood proudly over her table knowing that her cakes would be the first to sell out, just like they did every year.

As I watched her with pride, my mind wandered back to the day before.

As Aunt Dar was baking, I sat on the steps at the entrance of the kitchen, watching her stir the ingredients with a large wooden spoon. The last time she baked, after she put the contents into the cake tins, she gave me what was left in the mixer bowl to enjoy. It was delicious. I was looking forward to the same experience but when I asked for the bowl, she gave me a blank stare and carried on scraping the contents into the cake tins.

When the mouth-watering cakes were baked, I watched as she took them out of the oven.

I asked her for a slice but this time she was irritated by my persistence and shouted, "No!"

Later, when they were baked, she put them to cool on the counter and left the kitchen.

Obsessed with having cake, I was determined to take a slice, but I knew I would have to think of a way to do it without her noticing. So, when she wasn't looking, I climbed up onto the kitchen counter.

I removed the first in the row of six cakes from the tin by turning it upside down. With a straight-edged knife, I pared a thin layer from the bottom and ate it. It tasted just as delicious as it smelt. Afterwards, I put the cake back in the tin. I did the same thing again with a second cake. After eating another pared slice from the bottom, I was satisfied.

The next day, back at the churchyard, customers rushed over to form a line to buy Aunt Dar's cake.

Aunt Dar proudly cut a slice for one of the customers. As she raised it to place on a napkin, she noticed my handiwork. Her face dropped in horror. She looked at her other cakes.

Two of her perfectly golden sponge cakes had a white bottom. They had obviously been trimmed as if they'd been burned. Bursting with anger, Aunt Dar called Uncle John over to look at what I had done. She knew I was the culprit and her look turned from anger to sadness.

My decision to have a piece of cake caused embarrassment for Aunt Dar and damaged the pride of the local lady dignitary that was my great-aunt. To be seen to produce flawed cakes was far too humiliating for Aunt Dar and Uncle John. They dealt with their embarrassment by deciding for Uncle John to take me home straight away.

As we drove home in silence, I knew I was in trouble. He took me inside the house and removed the leather belt that he was wearing. He put me over his knees and brought the belt up high above him then whipped my bottom, hard. It hurt but most of all it shocked me.

I knew why he was upset. Did I anticipate that he was going to beat me? No. Did he know any other way to make his point about me doing something wrong? I don't think so.

It was the first time that I was beaten and the only time he ever beat me.

I loved him, and he loved me, so I was utterly shocked. I felt hurt and guilty all at the same time. This was when I first started to feel insecure because I learnt that people who loved me could also cause me pain.

Although it didn't erase the wonderful past with my Uncle John, this event affected my love for him. Now my memories were tainted with the stain of this shocking act. It could never be undone.

On a Sunday, my Uncle John drove us to the open-air movie theatre to watch black and white films and get ice cream. But that long, winding road to Harbour View was terrifying. As we drove, I looked out of the window and saw a deep dark gully all the way around.

It always seemed to me that we drove too near the edge of the road. I was scared the car could fall into the gully, that deep gully we could see as we drove on that winding road.

The night after the beating was probably the first time that I dreamt that I fell down that gully. I woke up suddenly from the dream to stop myself falling.

*Phew! I am alright. I am safe.*

# Uncle John

One Friday evening about a year after the beating, Uncle John came home from work. As usual, he got out of the car and shouted out, "P-A-M." I ran to him and, after opening the gate, he lifted me into his arms. But this time I could see a strange woman sitting in his car.

I was still in his arms holding that day's treat when he walked over to Aunt Dar who was standing by the water basin under the mango tree.

He asked her to get some clean clothes ready because he was going away for the weekend to a place where only adults went. It was called Milk River Bath, a mineral spa in the parish of Clarendon, believed to cure a variety of ailments. Aunt Dar went inside to collect the clean clothes. I can still remember her face when she came out again. Her eyes were red and puffy as though she had been crying.

She was breathing heavily and let out a deep sigh as she handed the clothes to him. Later I found out that the mystery woman in the car was Aunt Dar's best friend.

The next day, while Uncle John was away at Milk River, Aunt Dar packed one suitcase for me and another for herself. They were lightly filled with clothes and a few toiletries as though we were going away for a weekend.

"Where are we going?" I asked.

"We're moving to live somewhere else, away from John," she replied.

"Moving where? I want to stay with Uncle John," I protested.

"You are my responsibility, you can't stay here without me. After all, he is not your relative, I am."

I had no choice but to follow.

Although it was her inherited money that she used to build the house we shared with Uncle John and his children, she left it all behind.

She felt shame that her image as a community role model was being brought down by Uncle John's continued philandering.

Everyone knew he had other women, but he had never before been brazen enough to drive one of them to Aunt Dar's gate and make it obvious that he was taking the woman away for the weekend.

That day, we moved to live in a house that Aunt Dar was building to rent out.

We hoped for Uncle John to come for us and Aunt Dar prayed for his conscience to compel him to beg for forgiveness and take us home. But he never came.

Aunt Dar used to ask me if I had seen him on my way to and from school. I wished I had. She told me he was living with the other woman now. At the time, it seemed to me that where we were living was a long way from our old house. I later realised it was less than half a mile away. I never saw my Uncle John again.

Life got hard for Aunt Dar without the day-to-day income from him, but she made sure life wasn't different for me. I had food, clothes, and a roof over my head. I walked to school, which was now nearer than before.

Most days there wasn't much to do but play in the yard alone. Although we had neighbours with many children, Aunt Dar did not approve of me mixing with children whose families she didn't know. We planted two new mango trees and watered them every day. In the afternoon, she taught piano lessons and sold bags of ice to local people from her refrigerator, a convenience only very few owned.

Aunt Dar would not sell the land she still owned in Orange Park to help her get by, so it was farmed by locals who gave her a contribution if they sold any crops. This was how she survived.

On what seemed to be many occasions, Aunt Dar went to see her family in St. Elizabeth, the place where she was born.

While she was away, I stayed with her friend Miss Sonia, who lived at the end of our lane. Miss Sonia had six children of varying ages. They were friends to play with, and the older girl sometimes plaited my hair. She styled it in a much more modern style than my great-aunt ever did. I was a happy girl of eight with long slender legs, quickly growing out of my favourite pink and white striped dress.

One day when with Miss Sonia, I climbed their cherry tree to get the ripe fruit at the top. I disturbed a wasps' nest. When Aunt Dar returned and saw my swollen face, she was so worried she took me to see the nurse. But I was more concerned about what the nurse would do, than about the wasp stings.

The nurse was Aunt Dar's friend, but she didn't like children. In the past, every time I was taken to see her for an injection, she slapped me to get me to calm down.

"Stop crying." Slap. "Stop screaming." Slap.

"Hold her hand still while I give her this injection," she'd insist.

Then Aunt Dar gripped my arm tightly until it was over. But the nurse's treatment always hurt more than any injection.

Although Aunt Dar could be strict with me, I knew she cared for me deeply. One day, when she was cooking, I was watching her as usual and asked,

"Aunt Dar, what will I be when I grow up?"

*Will I be a teacher like the nice ones at school who complimented me for knowing the answers to their questions? Or will I be a nurse? Hopefully not like the evil one at the clinic.*

"You will be whatever you want to be," Aunt Dar replied. "You are bright and quick enough to do anything you decide."

These words were powerful. I felt that there were no limits to what I could do.

She believed in me. It was in this moment I knew that I loved Aunt Dar.

After that, I heard her proudly telling her friends about me asking her this question.

She tried to teach me to play the piano, but I wasn't interested. It wasn't my thing. She often called me to watch her sew. I had no interest in this either. I was a child with my own ideas about the things I wanted to do. I was interested in climbing trees because at the top of the tree I could sit and look down at what was going on, planning what I would do next in my world.

At home, I only had two everyday chores. One was to empty the chamber pots and the other was to sweep the house. Nothing too onerous. Sometimes Aunt Dar would send me to the standpipe on the main road to fetch water for the two mango trees we had planted in the front of the yard.

These were my mango trees. I took pride in watching them grow every day. Any mangoes that grew were mine. If anyone wanted one, they'd have to ask me. I felt important having responsibility for making decisions like this.

One Saturday Aunt Dar left me for the day. Before she went, she told me to sweep out the house, lock up and put the key under the mat, then go to Miss Sonia, her friend where all the children lived.

The temptation to go and play was too much. I figured I would go to Miss Sonia first then come back and do the chores before Aunt Dar got home. *She would never know*. I was having so much fun that I lost track of time and my plan.

As it began to get dark, I heard Miss Sonia call out, "Pam, Aunt Dar is here asking for you."

"Okay Miss Sonia," I answered and ran home through the opening in the wire fence at the side of Miss Sonia's house. Panting as I ran, my plan was to get home before my Aunt and quickly sweep the house. When I got there, I saw that she had already been home, the shopping bags were in the kitchen.

I hadn't seen her pass Miss Sonia's house! Aunt Dar must have walked home from the other end of the lane.

My heart pounded as she arrived. She was angry because the neighbour's cat got into the house before I locked the door. The stupid cat had defecated several times in the house. The smell!

She berated me and said she was going to give me a good hiding. I decided she had to catch me first. I was a fast runner. My natural flight instinct was triggered and, when I saw the belt, off I ran.

My aunt followed. I ran around the outside of the house as she chased me. I was sure I was fast and smart enough to outwit her. I anticipated that when she stopped, I would double back. I had no thought that this cat and mouse game would eventually have to end. She got smart on the third or fourth time, she stood still and I found myself running toward her instead of away from her.

That was when she picked up the stone and threw it. It caught me on the ankle and stopped me in my tracks. I still have the mark. That was the end of that assault. She broke my skin, drawing blood, which stopped her.

After a while, she called me, so she could look at the wound. She wiped away the blood then placed a plaster over the cut. She had hurt me but, soon after, was caring for me.

*Why did these adults that loved me hurt me too?*

Aunt Dar had friends with children around my age, who became my friends. When playing with the children, I overheard Aunt Dar talking with their mothers. "I've always had Pam, I'm the only mother she's ever known."

"Poor ting," they replied. "She nuh even know ar madda."

*I don't have a mother?* I thought. *Is it a bad thing? Is this something I should be upset about? Why didn't I know this before?*

Over time, I pieced together stories about my mother leaving Jamaica for America and taking my four elder siblings with her. I didn't know anything about her apart from her name – Rosita. Aunt Dar didn't say why I was left behind. I used to wonder why I didn't go with her.

*Didn't she want me? Will she come to get me one day?*

Up until now, as far as I was concerned, I'd lived with the people who represented my mother and father even though I didn't call them by that name.

It was after this that I started to imagine how my mother looked and what she might be like. I daydreamed about the mother I wanted to have. I pictured her coming to see me. She was a beautiful woman with long flowing hair, dressed in a pink American-style dress, the same colour as my favourite dress. I imagined her opening the gate and walking up to the veranda where Aunt Dar was sitting.

"Where's Pam?" She would ask.

I envisioned myself crouching behind Aunt Dar's chair staring at her, listening and marvelling at her American accent, and how pretty she looked. I saw myself waiting for her to speak to me, to call me over, to hold my hand. I fantasised repeatedly hoping that one day my dream would finally come true.

# Plans to Escape

As time went on, Aunt Dar's temper seemed to quicken, and she became visibly annoyed at even the smallest things. She always moaned about my father, who she said lived in England. I didn't know anything about him apart from what she told me. Apparently, he didn't regularly send money to look after me. He did on a few occasions, but she said it was nowhere near enough.

For a while, Aunt Dar worked at the house of a local wealthy man. She was his housekeeper but didn't want anyone to know about this, as she was embarrassed. The man was amorous towards her, but she wasn't interested in him. Many years later, she told me that she didn't think it was worth giving herself to someone whom she didn't like in that way, just to have a financially easier life.

Aunt Dar soon became so frustrated with all her money worries that she wanted to escape, to get away from Jamaica and move to America.

One day I heard her tell her friends, "Pam's mother is arranging for both of us to join her in America where I'll be looking after her. She's started to take out the papers to sponsor us."

She was so animated when she said this, almost boasting. Going to America was the best thing anyone could hope for. It was a chance to work and get good pay, guaranteed food and a good life, which was extremely hard to achieve in Jamaica.

The American dream was revered. Going to Britain was the second-best option. For Aunt Dar, this would put her in an even better economic position than when she was living with Uncle John. It was another thing that would make her superior to her friends.

Then one day, some months later, Aunt Dar was on the veranda with her friends. I was sitting on the floor of the living room which led onto the veranda, playing a game of 'Jacks', where you bounce a small ball and speedily pick up small six-pronged metal pieces before the ball hits the ground.

What I heard made me stop playing my game.

Aunt Dar told her friends that my mother died of cancer.

"Poor Pam, never know ar madda, and now she die, poor ting," they cried.

But I didn't know how I was supposed to feel.

*Am I supposed to feel sad that she is dead? Am I never to get to know this person they call my mother?*

Aunt Dar never spoke directly to me about my mother's death. However, it was then that I realised my dream could never come true. My mother had died, leaving me forever.

Our passports had to be obtained quickly so we could attend her funeral. Aunt Dar got her passport in time, but mine didn't come. There was a problem with the paperwork. Aunt Dar couldn't have gone without me, so we missed the funeral.

Aunt Dar was deeply upset. She felt that she had lost her opportunity to escape her current life. I or, at least, my mother's funeral was to be her ticket out of Jamaica, but it was taken away from her by the passport office!

I was disappointed that I missed the chance to go on an aeroplane and visit America. I wasn't going to know my fantasy mother either.

*Does this mean that I will never meet my brothers and sisters, and do I have to stay in Jamaica with Aunt Dar forever?*

# Where's the Money?

After my mother died, life carried on, but my Aunt Dar was still distressed and gradually withdrew from me.

One evening when I was around nine, I came running home from school. I entered the gate and walked through the yard to the front of the house. My great-aunt was sitting on the veranda with a neutral smile.

"Good evening Aunt Dar," I chirped.

"Pam, go change out of your school uniform and come here," she instructed.

"Yes, Aunt Dar," I replied and off I went to my room.

When I came back dressed in my house clothes, I stood in front of her, on the veranda, wondering what task she was going to ask me to do.

Suddenly, she grabbed my wrists.

"What did I do?" I gasped.

My mind raced.

*Did I forget to take out the chamber pots this morning? Is she going to tell me off for not sweeping my room? Is she going to hit me? The moment she lets go, I'm going to run. She can't catch me.*

"Pam, why did you steal the money?"

*What did she say?* I thought. *Why is she asking me about money? What money?*

"You took the money that I got from selling your father's land," she blurted out. "He told me to sell the land and give half to that Daisy Johnson woman, the woman he had a son with when he was with your mother and I was to keep half to look after you. You stole it!"

"What, Aunt Dar?" I asked, stunned.

*What is she talking about, what money?*

My mouth was open, but nothing was coming out. The words were trapped in my throat. I couldn't make sense of the accusation. My mind just didn't understand.

"Where...is... the... money?" Aunt Dar insisted.

"What money?" I stuttered.

She reached down under her chair for a piece of thick rubber hose, a metre long, that she must have cut earlier.

*Oh my God! Is she really going to beat me with that?*

The grip on my wrist tightened. She struck me with such speed and force that the pain was delayed.

"Tell me what you did with the money!" she demanded.

"What money, Aunt Dar? I didn't do anything!"

The lashings continued in a frenzied indiscriminate attack on my back, my side, my bottom, my legs. In between the pain and shock of the allegation, I could hardly speak.

As tears rolled down my cheeks, all I could do was repeat, "What money, Aunt Dar?"

Whack! Whack! Whack! Whack! Whack! I tried to wrestle away from her clutch, but the pain was debilitating.

She loosened her grip for a millisecond as she tried to adjust her hold on me and I snatched my hand away. As she regained her balance, I ran down the two veranda steps. Then she swung at me, catching my hip with the end of the hose.

I headed straight to the back of the house. I looked behind me, but she was on my heels, closer than I thought. I was terrified, so I gathered speed.

Because of her high blood pressure, she was getting out of breath and slowing down, complaining of a headache.

"You're going to give me a stroke," she panted as she gasped for air.

Despite the pain in my legs from the beating, I ran to the overgrown, derelict yard behind our house.

Colin, Aunt Dar's errand man, was walking by the house.

"Colin, come help me find Pam," she cried.

"Yes, Miss Dar, where she gaan?

"Round the back, go find her."

So, Colin tried to locate me. From my hiding place in an old rusty drum lying on its side, I overheard them in the distance calling out my name. I kept still so they couldn't find me. I was petrified and felt hopeless.

*Oh my God! What just happened? What am I going to do?*

Running to another yard to ask for help was not an option. I was always told not to involve other people in our private business. It wouldn't help anyway, because they beat their children too.

After about an hour, I fell asleep with exhaustion, still inside the drum. I was too afraid to sleep outside in the dark, so I decided to walk back to the house. There was nowhere else to go, no sanctuary, no one to rescue me.

The back door was open, so I quietly snuck into my room and got into bed. I could still hear Aunt Dar talking to Colin at the front of the house before I dozed off.

The next morning, she dragged me out of bed and into the kitchen. I saw the dreaded green hose leaning against the wall in the corner of the kitchen.

She placed my breakfast on the table in front of me without saying a word.

*Did my running away calm her down?*

I ate the food as she watched from where she was leaning on the sink.

Then the questioning started again.

"Pam, tell me what you did with the money?"

"What money, Aunt Dar? I don't know anything about any money."

"Pam, I heard the shopkeeper next to your school said a lot of money was spent in her shop last week. Did you take my money and give it to someone at school?"

"No, Aunt Dar," I replied. "I didn't take any money, I didn't give it to anybody at school."

She was irritated by my denial and grabbed the hose. The beating started again.

*Oh, please God, make her stop. I don't know what to do to get her to stop. Help!*

"I know you took the money, do not lie to me," she screamed.

"I'm not lying, Aunt Dar, I didn't take it," I whimpered between each lashing.

"You did. You took it, admit it," she insisted.

Whack! Whack! Whack!

*Is she trying to kill me?*

"Well," she declared, "We are going to the shop to ask Miss Riley."

*A break from the beating, thank you, God!*

Before walking with her to the shop, I washed my face and got dressed. My body was still burning from the pain. The welts were disguised under my dress, but the blood stains weren't.

As we walked, I passed my friends who had just seen me getting beaten at the house.

Knowing that they saw me as having a privileged life, the embarrassment of being publicly shamed was overwhelming.

We arrived at Miss Riley's shop. She was sat behind the counter waiting for customers.

"Good afternoon, Miss Riley," said Aunt Dar. "I hear that you were saying school children had extra money to spend in your shop last week. Is that true?"

I was standing behind Aunt Dar watching the conversation, frightened that Miss Riley might say yes.

I was relieved when Miss Riley replied. "No, Miss Dar."

After the wasted journey, we walked back home. I don't know why Aunt Dar kept up this farce and was so intent on blaming me for something I didn't do.

When we got home, my aunt picked up the hose again.

*Oh God, more beating!*

"Who did you give the money to?" she cried, weary and exhausted but still beating me.

I was tired, defeated, and my spirit broken. My ears were ringing, and I couldn't see clearly. My mind was spinning, I was passing in and out of consciousness.

*What do I say? What can I do? Am I about to die?*

Finally, Aunt Dar let me go to bed and I quickly fell asleep.

It was morning, a new day and my great-aunt had a new idea about the missing money.

"Why don't you admit it?" she said, eyeing me calmly. "You gave it to one of your little friends, didn't you?"

I denied the accusation, yet again and she beat me, again!

"You must have given it to someone, so give me a name and it will stop."

*Who can I say has it? Will this really stop?*

The only person's name that I could come up with was my best friend, Rose Brown. "Rose, Aunt Dar, Rose Brown."

"Go and get ready. We are going to her house, I know where she lives!" Aunt Dar commanded.

I had met Rose at school. She was the same age as me, and we used to compete to answer the teacher's questions in class. We went to the same church, we played together, and we found the same things funny. I liked her more than anyone else, she was my very best friend.

Aunt Dar and I walked a mile until we got to Rose's house behind our church.

"Hello," Aunt Dar said casually to the people she knew as we made our way.

I was exhausted, but at least this was better than the beating. Yet all I could think was,

*What have I done? Have I just condemned Rose to the same fate as me?*

We got to the gate of Rose's house and Aunt Dar called out to Rose's mother. They were in the choir group together so were familiar with each other.

"Yes, Miss Dar," Rose's mother greeted her. "Hello, how are you?"

"Pam stole my money and gave it to your daughter," Aunt Dar stated.

The expression on Rose's mother's face changed from joy at having a guest, to concern. She called out to Rose, who came running over, smiling, happy to see me. She bent down, held Rose's hand and looked her in the eye,

"Did Pam give you any money?"

Rose thought I had come to play with her, so she took a few seconds to respond to her mother.

"No mommy."

Rose's mother knew that she was telling the truth and hugged her. It was clear that she was defending her daughter. Seeing Rose and her mother so close to each other, made me feel alone. I had no one on my side, no one to hug me.

Aunt Dar said goodbye and led me silently back to our house. After returning home, there was no explanation or discussion, but the beatings finally stopped. Her communication with me went back to normal as if the accusations and violence had never happened.

Life continued but I was a changed person, subdued. I went to school not as confident as before, living with the embarrassment of being branded a thief. It was a shame that I carried with me for years.

# America

A year later, when I was ten, my uncle and siblings arranged for me to join them in New York. They ensured the completion of the immigration process and sent a cousin who was visiting Jamaica from America, to help sort out the passport and to buy the air ticket.

Now, Aunt Dar wasn't to come with me. I never found out why. After the beatings, I wasn't sad to leave her or Jamaica. I just liked the idea of being in an aeroplane, like the ones I had watched overhead for years as I fantasised that my mother was coming to get me. I was finally heading to meet my family. They had come to my rescue at last.

And so, I left Jamaica on a summer's day in June 1970. I sat in the cold cabin for eight hours, feeling the chill of the air-conditioning that I had never experienced before.

On landing at JFK Airport, I was looked after by the stewardess who also ushered me to the arrivals gate.

There, I was greeted by some new and strange people who were my sister Loretta and Uncle Alfredo.

"Hi Pam," they said.

"Hello," I muttered, overawed but excited by the newness of the situation. I followed them as they took my bag to the car.

We drove on roads that seemed to me to be at least two times the size of the ones I had driven on in Jamaica. We passed gigantic buildings before stopping in Brooklyn and parking in front of one of the large family houses. The houses were joined together, there was no land between them like there was in Jamaica. When we went inside, there were more people who I had never seen before. They were my other brother and sister.

My Uncle Alfredo, who was proud to own the house, lived downstairs in the basement apartment.

My room was on the top floor. It used to be my mother's bedroom before she died. Her perfume was still on the dressing table in a candlestick shaped bottle. Above the fireplace was a picture of my older sister, Loretta, the one who met me at the airport. It seemed that she was the head of the household, although she didn't live there all the time.

Loretta stood at approximately five feet, two inches tall, with a flawless brown complexion. Her hair was cut short, shaped perfectly to suit her face. She had brown eyes, a mole on her left cheek and a smile that pulled you in. To me, this combination made her beautiful.

There were four siblings in total. Roberto was the eldest who visited but didn't live with us. He was followed by Loretta, who was engaged to be married, then Tony who seemed more preoccupied with his friends and our extended family members than with any of us. Veronica followed, she was quiet and petite with model looks.

I was happy to meet them for the first time although a little bewildered and in awe. I could see that they all had a relationship, a bond with each other and something in common. I didn't have that with them. I was the outsider, the stranger.

My new family made sure my basic needs for food, clothes and shelter, were met but they were busy people living their lives. Whenever my brother Tony was around, he popped his head into my room and said, "You alright?"

"Yes!" I'd answer, smiling and waiting for the rest of the conversation but it didn't follow.

He was usually just popping in and acknowledging me, before running off to do something else, taking his positive energy with him.

On occasions, Tony asked me to sew a button on for him, which I knew how to do from having watched Aunt Dar back in Jamaica. He also asked me to shine his shoes while he talked to one of his friends as he got dressed to go out with them again.

Apart from these interactions with Tony on the few occasions he was at home, the family rarely spoke to me. I can only remember one time when Loretta and I actually came close to having a conversation.

We were all having dinner when Loretta announced, "Aunt Dar was a cruel woman." I stopped eating, desperate for her to say more. "One time, when you were a baby, we stayed with her for a week," Loretta explained. "When I came home from school in the evenings, the first thing that old witch did was make me wash all your dirty diapers. She put them to soak in the basin and left them for me even though there were helpers who could wash them!" Loretta peered at me and asked, "Did you have anything to do with that Johnson woman, the one our father had an affair with?"

I didn't reply but she kept probing.

"Isn't she living with him in England now? What about that son of theirs, our half-brother Oliver, where is he?"

I didn't know the answers to her questions. The only thing I knew about our father's mistress was her name because Aunt Dar had said she gave her half of the money from the sale of our father's land. The other half of the money is what Aunt Dar accused me of taking.

I didn't know what to say but she just kept looking at me. In the end, I just said, "Yes," and that was the end of the conversation. Loretta never asked me anything about the beatings in Jamaica or my experience of Aunt Dar.

But the sisters had conversations with each other about me within my earshot.

I overheard Loretta telling Veronica, "She's growing fast, she needs a dress coat and she'll need new shoes…"

In the early days, I sat in the bedroom looking around or listening to them talk. I didn't really know what to do, where I could sit or what I could say. I couldn't join in, because children never took part in adult conversations.

My new family weren't indifferent, but they didn't give me the attention I needed. There was never a time when they sat down and talked to me about what I wanted or how I felt. This wasn't something they did with me. Perhaps they did not understand that I, a stranger, needed to be talked to and asked questions, as a relationship was what I desperately craved. Their unspoken understanding, which developed from their time together since birth, was not there for me. I did not grow with them.

It seemed to me that the only direct communication, and the only time my name was called, was to be chastised.

Any communication was always an accusation or a statement, never a conversation that could bring Lorretta or me to an understanding.

I was too timid to try to speak to them even though I wanted to be part of the conversations, to be accepted as part of the family. And we didn't do hugs in that household, so any accidental physical contact as we went about our day to day lives felt strange to me.

I was afraid of Loretta because she was so inaccessible to me and always seemed quite angry. I wouldn't have known how to talk to her even if she wanted to.

One morning, I woke up and headed for the bathroom still half asleep. As I approached the open door, I saw Loretta standing in front of the mirror, half-dressed and putting on her make-up.

When she saw me, she screamed, "Get back to goddam bed. What are you doing up?"

She was full of a venom that I can't forget, even to this day. But now I realise I had interfered in one of the few moments she had for herself.

My New York family never spoke to me about our mother; who she was, what she looked like, nothing. I didn't ask about her because it seemed a forbidden subject. There were no pictures of her around either. They seemed to be a family that didn't talk about emotional things.

Sometimes Loretta arranged for Veronica to take me on shopping trips to buy clothes. In Jamaica, we didn't shop in this way. We had a dressmaker who made our clothes and, if you were lucky, there would be ready-made clothes sent by family members who lived abroad.

The first time I ever travelled on a train was to go shopping in New York. We walked a short distance from our house in Brooklyn, then we arrived at the station. I had never seen a train before. It was wonderful and scary. Veronica held my hand as we got off one train and changed to the next, ending up in Manhattan, where giant buildings loomed and there were lots of people from different backgrounds. All of them walking fast, talking to each other with American accents and in other languages I didn't understand. In the big shops we visited, Veronica chose what seemed to me to be an inordinate amount of new clothes.

"Try this on," she said.

I tried on tops, trousers, skirts, one after the other. Veronica enjoyed shopping. I was overwhelmed yet happy about getting new clothes.

Loretta sometimes arranged for Veronica to take me to the movies, or to Broadway where I saw musicals such as 'The Wizard of Oz' and 'Hansel and Gretel.' Veronica also took me to gospel shows in Harlem, full of African Americans. The powerful singers and music penetrated my mind, body, and soul, creating an energy that was totally consuming and contagious. You couldn't help but be happy in this environment.

On one occasion, Loretta and her husband Clay even took me out themselves. We went to Times Square to see a Michael Jackson concert. I fell in love with Michael that evening. He was going to be my husband. I even planned our wedding as I watched the show!

Although these actions reflected Loretta's laudable intention to stretch beyond meeting my basic needs, she still didn't attempt to develop a relationship with me.

Even though she was my sister-cum-mother, she didn't realise that what I needed most was a connection with her, with them, with something.

I needed her understanding, her words. If only she knew what I wanted most was positive communication with her.

I often looked at her, wanting her to like me. But she just seemed to be irritated by my silent adoration.

It was hard for her. Her mother, to whom she was very close, had not long died and she had to take over the household. She was only twenty-one, eleven years older than me. She planned to get married and have her own children.

Now, she was forced to pursue her plans without help and had her mother's youngest child to look after. One that needed a lot of care because she was little, estranged from the family and had suffered trauma.

I once heard Loretta tell Veronica that she literally helped to bring me into this world. One day, back in Jamaica, she went home for lunch and found my mother amid childbirth. She helped the midwife with all she had to do to bring me safely into the world.

Now she had to care for me full time. She had no time to grieve for our mother's loss, she just had to 'suck it up' and live with what life dealt her. Emotions! Who had time for those? Is it any wonder that she was never happy?

However, my sister Veronica guided me through puberty very well. One summer's evening, I returned indoors after sitting on the outside steps of the house. I was wearing a beige dress with a beautiful multi-coloured band around the waist.

After watching me walk in, Veronica called out, "Pam, come here." When I turned around, she picked up the hem of my dress and asked me to have a look.

It had a red stain on the back. "Follow me into the bathroom," she whispered. I didn't know what to feel, half thinking that I may have done something wrong. But from her attitude, it didn't seem like she wanted to chastise me.

When we got into the bathroom, she ran the bath and told me to get in. When I did, I saw that there was blood on my panties.

After my bath, she handed me a towel and sat on the closed toilet seat as I dried myself.

With a thick white padded rectangle in her hand, she said, "Pam, this is called a sanitary towel, for when you have your period every month. You'll have to use these until it stops, so it doesn't make a mess of your clothes."

Veronica showed me how to put it on, including how to use the belt we had in those days, to hold it in place. After telling me where they were kept and that I could use what I needed every month, Veronica left the bathroom. I didn't ask any questions, it was bewildering but also a special moment between us. It could have been the perfect moment for her to talk to me about sex or pregnancy, but those important things went unsaid.

Before long, I met new members of my family too. I met uncles who had children and discovered that I have a lot of cousins! It seemed that each uncle had at least eight children. Some of them I met and liked. Prince, a teenage distant cousin, spent time with me and talked to me a lot. He asked me about my old life.

"Pam, tell me about Jamaica," he said, listening patiently as I described my life there, the good and the bad. One day, I told him about the beatings.

With tears running down his face, he shook his head and said, "I hate her, I want to kill her," and held my hand as I spoke. I loved him for this.

Prince and I talked for hours, often forgetting to eat. Sometimes we talked so long that it was too late for him to go home, so he slept on the sofa.

He told me about his mother, which fed my hunger to know about my family. I looked forward to him coming to see me, which my family didn't seem to mind, especially as they weren't home.

However, one day while we were talking, my uncle called him downstairs. I don't know what happened but after that, I never saw him again! We lost touch, and years ago I heard that he died. I miss him even now.

# New York

I arrived in New York in the summer of 1970 and started school in September. I was the 'Jamaican girl' that's how the American children saw me. Loretta sent me for speech therapy to 'sort out' my slight lisp, improve my pronunciation and change my accent, with a view to helping me assimilate quicker.

In Jamaica, we children admired the American accent, believing anything was better than our own. So, when I met the speech therapist, because I admired how she spoke and because she gave me attention, I took in everything she said. I still remember the repeated effort to pronounce the letter 'S' and to put my tongue between my teeth for 'Th.'

It seemed to me that it was very important to Loretta that we wiped out the memory of Jamaica, particularly the accent. I don't know why. Perhaps it was because she felt I would have more advantages in life if I assimilated well or perhaps she wanted to block out how difficult life was for her in Jamaica.

I happily went to my junior high school, a place I liked. There was only one thing that I didn't like; three of the popular American girls (bigger than me in size but the same age) sometimes teased me about my Jamaican accent.

My reaction? Well, there was a marked difference between the girl in Jamaica before the beating and the girl I now was. I no longer fought back readily, with either my mouth or my fist. I was not a doormat, so they didn't go all out with their teasing, but I was not a fighter either and they knew it. I already had a sense of defeat before tackling all of life's little battles.

Fortunately, the school environment gave me respite from home. The classes were not difficult, what was difficult was just focusing on what I was being taught. Half of my mind was bewildered by all that was new to me; the country, family and my relationships at home. Not to mention that part of me the earlier beatings had dulled, the questions that I could not ask, and the feelings that I had about being unwanted and unloved.

With so much going on, I squeezed in some learning, and incredibly, quite a lot stuck. I can still remember the details of American history, the Civil War and the American version of World War II.

School in America was different from Jamaica. The teachers' approach wasn't as strict. Back home, the teachers were competent in imparting knowledge. They believed deeply in the value of education and knew it was the way out of poverty for their students. They were so desperate to impart this, they beat us into conformity, into behaving. I don't believe they knew any other way to get good behaviour.

In Jamaica, the cane and leather belts were the tools of discipline. When children were late, the Head Teacher or Deputy Head stood at the gate waving a thick leather belt to catch as many of them as possible, hitting them as they ran into school. A school friend of mine used to avoid going in if he was late, and he was frequently. He often hid in the big mango tree near the old bridge by the river rather than go in to be hit.

In America, there was no violence meted out by teachers. We, the children, could even laugh with teachers. Another difference was, in Jamaica we wore school uniforms but in America, we wore our own clothes. I was one of the children that were age-appropriately dressed in a simple blouse, woollen top and skirt or trousers.

Confident girls, including the ones who teased me, wore trendy bell bottom pants, with tight tops, and shoes with thick high heels, the type of clothes my teenage sister Veronica wore. There were girls who were considered average and others who were considered 'on trend' because of what they wore. I was not 'on trend.' In Jamaica, the competition between the girls was about whose pleats were the sharpest on the skirt, whose uniform was the least washed out, the newest. A well-kept uniform meant you understood how hard it was for your parents to afford to buy the material and get the uniform made. It meant that you had a good upbringing. Things like this also made you a good child and, of course, so did obedience.

My junior high school building was enormous in comparison to my little school in Jamaica. The teachers in America were a balance of male and female. In Jamaica, all my teachers were female, including my Head Teacher. In America, my favourite teacher in junior high was Mr Shiparo. He was a Jewish man with very wide hips (I noticed them because it was so unusual). He also had a straight, large, narrow nose that made me wonder how he could breathe. Why was he my favourite? He was pleasant and kind to all the children. He was interested in what we had to say. He made learning fun. He seemed to love his subjects, and that made me love them too. He told jokes that made the whole class and himself laugh. He got me involved in music classes and, while we were practising for a performance of Dionne Warwick's songs I discovered I was an alto. I still know those songs now.

Like all children, I just wanted to fit in. Perhaps my sister-mother Loretta understood the importance of this, hence the speech classes.

One time, after I heard my sisters talking about how they did not tolerate anyone picking on them, I told Veronica about the teasing that I was experiencing at school. She asked me where these bullies lived. I knew where the leader of this teasing trio lived because I passed her home on the way to and from school every day, worrying that she might come out just as I walked by.

The next day, we went to the girl's house together. Veronica told that member of the trio in no uncertain terms to stop teasing me and warned what she would do to her if she ever did it again. That was the end of that, there was no more teasing or bullying from the girl and her little gang. That incident became the foundation that binds Veronica and me together to this day. Rescuing me would win my love every time.

I longed to look like the trendy girls at school. One day, looking through the drawers of a dressing table in my bedroom, I saw Veronica's sparkly new tops and tried them on. They were fashionable, similar to what the most popular girls in school wore. I wore one to school that day, trying to look like an all-American girl. When I got home, I took it off and put it back in the drawer, being careful to fold it back precisely, or so I thought.

Of course, Veronica found out. The drama! Her reaction! Veronica telephoned Loretta, saying, "Do you know what she did? She wore my new top to school and put it back, trying to hide that she wore it!"

Loretta called me to the phone. I took a deep breath as she asked me what the hell was wrong with me. Oh, the cussing!

My sisters found a unity against their common enemy – me. I knew the next time sister-mother came around, I was in trouble.

I thought that Veronica was not a friend. She could defend me on one occasion then betray me on another. I guess that's the way all siblings feel about each other from time to time.

Another time at home, bored, as usual, I decided to go looking through all the drawers in the dressing table in my room. I found money in one of the drawers. After that, I occasionally took a few dollars. Having money to buy things like the other school children felt good. I could buy cakes and sweets from the shops. Did I think about the consequences? No. I thought about the happiness I got from having it. I was like some of the other children. Having buying power meant inclusion with the 'in-crowd'.

When Loretta found out about the money, she was livid. Apparently, it was her savings towards her wedding.

"Pam, come here," she cried.

"Yes Loretta," I answered as I shuffled toward her, afraid.

"I said come here," she yelled, yanking me towards her. "You thief, you took my money. Why did you take it?"

Bitterness emanated from her. I couldn't answer, all I could do was look down, wringing my hands.

I suspect she automatically assumed it was I who took the money because, after all, I had been accused of stealing before. I think she may have believed I took the money my great-aunt wrongly accused me of stealing.

I had no idea what the money in the dressing table was for or to whom it belonged. I can't describe the thought process that resulted in me taking the money, perhaps because there wasn't one. From my vantage point, the money was there, and I took some.

And so, I was labelled a thief, again.

There were no attempts to understand why I took the money. The adult was hurt, and I had caused it. I was a bad person.

Loretta's response was to try to kill me, at least that's what it felt like at the time. She called me into the kitchen to tell me off again, grabbing a wooden handled broom in her rage. I don't remember how we ended up at the top of the stairs, perhaps because I was trying to get away, that flight instinct of mine kicking in again.

My goodness was Loretta mad. Each blow was accompanied by her angry words.

"You bitch!" Whack! "You thief!" Whack! "What's wrong with you?" Whack!

She lifted the broomstick and hit me with it again and again. I raised my hand to block the blows, but the broomstick slammed into my face, breaking the delicate skin under my eye. The mark was visible for many years. If you look closely enough, you can still see it even now.

Was Loretta so crazed that she didn't consider that the broomstick could have blinded me? Again, another frustrated adult venting on the most vulnerable target.

At the time, I didn't understand the issues. I didn't have a relationship with her and the lack of direct communication had left us in this situation. She must have been so put out by the fact that she had to support me and now this. It made her feel insulted, that despite her efforts she wasn't appreciated. Her quest for freedom from her parent's responsibilities was being thwarted by her baby sister taking her money.

It was a symbol of how unfair her life was. Every time she felt she was moving forward, she was blocked, first with her mother dying then me having to live with them. And then I take money from her? She wanted to kill someone and that someone was me.

When she stopped hitting me and was sitting in the kitchen moaning to Veronica, I took the opportunity to escape. I was worried about her hitting me again, and no one stopping her.

With my heart thumping and my head spinning, I slowly crept down the stairs. I didn't know where I was going, I just knew I had to get away.

When I got outside, I walked and walked. Eventually, I stopped at a church. I pushed open the great big wooden door. It was empty, there was no one else there. I went to lay down on one of the rock-hard wooden pews. It was much more comfortable than being at home with my family.

I slept until I was woken up by the priest.

"Where do you live little lady?" he asked.

I told him.

"You should go home, won't your mother be worrying about you?"

I didn't want to explain anything, so I remained silent. He encouraged me to go home, and I left the church and went back home some hours later. Where else could I go?

When I returned, Veronica immediately telephoned Loretta who had gone to her place. She was angry and may even have been afraid for herself and for me after the beating she had given me.

But after the attack, the alienation continued. This included them treating me as the evil sister at Loretta's wedding. No bridesmaid's dress for me, the pariah, the bad one, the one that sister-mother hated.

Even my three other uncles that I never met before were alerted to this 'stealing money' incident. But Uncle Fidel showed that he cared. He took me to the cinema, bought me some popcorn and said, "Never mind, Pam. You weren't to know."

To this day I value his kindness. Those few words were like gold to me. I needed to hear them. Sadly, I didn't get to tell him how much I appreciated his kindness before he died. The other two uncles made it known that they cared too but in less verbal ways. They called my name in a loving way and still gave me treats. One of them gave me a hug when he was standing in the kitchen, listening to them describe what I did and how angry they were with me.

Again, these problems were created by an intense lack of communication. I did not know what life was like for my siblings. They didn't say. I only had what I imagined before coming to see them and what I imagined while living with them. I guess they assumed I knew how life was for them. I also thought they knew how things were for me, without me needing to say. Sister-mother Loretta sometimes asked, "Why did you do that?" "Why do you do this?" or "What's wrong with you?"

I had no idea what she expected back.

It is only now that I appreciate that Loretta had needs of her own.

Up to now, I have been resentful and unable to see the frustrations that she expressed through her behaviour towards me, the most vulnerable in the household. I hope Loretta had someone to speak to. I hope she shared with her husband, with someone, just how life was for her.

I recently found a letter she wrote to our father. I felt the pain she expressed and her sense of loneliness, believing there was no one to help her.

Around this point, I started to run away regularly. I can't remember how many times. When I did, I ran from something. It wasn't without reason. It wasn't because I was bad or evil and wanted to cause people distress. It was because I was frightened and upset.

Rather than go home late or face the consequences of some minor misdemeanour, I stayed out usually walking around the neighbourhood.

It was better to get respite, to have some peace instead of going home to that uncommunicative, negative environment. It was also a sterile existence; school, homework, sleep, eat, do not watch the television, do not do anything unless they decided I could.

Sometimes I just felt overwhelmed, wondering what else I might've done wrong that I wasn't aware of.

*What will sister-mother say next? What will she do? What will Uncle Alfredo say? Am I sitting on the chair in the wrong way? Am I looking at them without conveying contriteness? Will everything I do just be wrong?*

Existing in their midst, there was always a problem. Leaving the house gave me other things to be interested in. It gave me freedom from my plight, or so I thought.

# Brooklyn

As I was often home alone, I amused myself by watching TV. I used to watch lots of Batman, John Wayne and Mae West movies. I sat in front of the TV, half-waiting for my guardian Uncle Alfredo, whose apartment was in the basement.

I used to listen out for his footsteps coming up the stairs, but he always appeared quicker than I expected. When I heard the stairs creak as he took the first step, I'd jump up to turn off the TV. Often his long legs meant he could straddle two steps at a time and before I knew it, he was in the living room.

When I was successful, he found me with a book by my side, pretending not to have watched TV. The book was always at the ready just in case he turned up.

Sometimes he touched the TV set feeling for the heat that proved that it had been on. Depending on his mood, sometimes he told me off, or once or twice I got the belt. On the rare occasion I watched it in his sight, he quizzed me about who the producer or director was and what the real names of the stars were. There was nothing more annoying. I didn't want to be studying and remembering anything to be tested later. I just wanted to enjoy the programmes.

I never watched television with my family – we didn't even watch the news. We never talked about what was going on in New York. There was no discussion about any dangers or how to keep myself safe.

In rural Jamaica, I was closeted away up to the age of ten. Thrust into my new home in Brooklyn, how was I supposed to know that I could encounter danger just from walking in my neighbourhood? 'Stranger danger' they call it now.

I had no idea. No one told me. I had never lived in an urban area where I may have picked up the need for the vigilance and caution that some city dwellers understand.

Most certainly, I was not aware at age twelve of the risk from the old white man who used to pull up in his car alongside me on the road from time to time.

I thought he was a nice man. He was kind to me, so different from what I had been experiencing. In Jamaica, I always heard that white people were good, and that the whiter you were, the better you were. This belief and need for kindness meant that I got into his car.

Other things happened to me in his car. This seemed to me to be the price I had to pay for the kind words he spoke to me. He met a need for attention and some sort, any sort, of recognition. He bought me things. He never shouted, we just chatted and drove.

Things developed gradually. First, he drove to an empty car park or a derelict area where we talked. He gave me soda pop and potato chips, which we shared.

Then, after a while, he taught me how to masturbate him. I had no idea what it meant or what it was about. This happened on a number of occasions over approximately six months. It only stopped when I no longer felt the need to escape from home.

What might have happened if I had carried on spending time with him? He saw my innocence and vulnerability and my need for connection and took advantage of it.

I didn't tell anyone about this. What would they say?

Despite or possibly because of this abuse, my own sexuality started to awaken around this time.

One day, I visited the home of a boy I knew from school. We had been talking in the evenings for a little while and flirting with each other, so going to his house seemed like a natural progression. I liked him, and he liked me.

That was the evening that I lost my virginity. Afterwards, I went home thinking about what just happened but being unable to speak to anyone about it. It was my secret. The boy and I saw each other at school after that but nothing happened between us again. No one had ever spoken to me about sex, using protection to prevent disease and pregnancy. I didn't know anything about that.

Life went on in that Brooklyn house. My sister Veronica was around then. She looked every inch the 1970's fashion model with her bell-bottom trousers, her big afro hair, and platform shoes. She listened to the likes of Ester Phillips, Marvin Gaye, and Aretha Franklin, these were always playing in the background as she cooked or got ready to go out.

This was a time in New York when the effects of the Black Power movement could be felt. African Americans, men and women, walked with a sense of defiance, confidence and swagger, vigorously expressing pride in being black. Veronica epitomised this with the way she dressed, the books she read and the conversations she had with her friends on the phone. I liked the energy it created in the house.

But then things changed when Veronica was thrown out by my uncle because she had a boyfriend. It was a cold winter's day, and she may have stayed out the night before. Sitting in my room, I heard my uncle call her downstairs and her loud sigh as she descended the stairs to see him. They argued and after a while, she came back upstairs.

I then heard the front door slam. I rushed to the window in the living room to see her open the gate and walk down the snow-filled road with her blanket under her arm.

She didn't say goodbye, she just left, leaving home and leaving me in that big house.

Oh, the strict rules! The standards! I now know one of the reasons our uncle may have been so stern. It must have been his way of managing the range of responsibilities he had for his sister's children, his way of coping with such a heavy burden.

My elder brother Roberto was already living somewhere else and the newly married Loretta no longer visited frequently. Tony was almost never home now.

I never felt forgiven for taking the money. Every time I saw Loretta, she was so angry it was as if I had committed the crime that very day.

Finally, she became so frustrated that she took me to see a social worker. We arrived at the skyscraper in Manhattan and took the lift to the eighth floor.

When we reached the reception, Loretta asked for Mrs Rebecca Rosen. After a few minutes, she came out to greet us. Mrs Rosen was around thirty-five years old, tall and slim, wearing a long skirt that reached her ankles. She had slightly bulging eyes, an oval shaped face and a gentle manner.

"Hello," she said, offering her hand. Loretta shook it and I followed, shyly. "Come in, sit down," she smiled. "Would you like something to drink?"

"No thank you," Loretta replied.

Mrs Rosen looked at me, kindly. "Pam, do you want something to drink?"

"No thank you," I whispered.

Then we went into her office, which was beautiful. There were windows all around the room providing a wonderful view of the sky and surrounding buildings. Her desk was made of orange wood. She sat behind it and we sunk into the comfortable, soft chairs facing her.

Mrs Rosen asked Loretta to tell her about my history and what was going on. After explaining how I came from Jamaica to live with them, Loretta said,

"We do everything for her, yet she steals and runs away. I don't know what to do. I think there is something wrong with her."

As I listened, I started to feel hopeless. Then Loretta left to return to work, saying my brother Tony would pick me up.

I was upset that Loretta had said there was something wrong with me. Mrs Rosen knew it and came to sit near me. She asked me questions about school and about the things I liked to do. She said things like, "Tell me what happened when...", "How did you feel?" And, "What did you think about ..."

Thereafter, every week for around six months, I went to see the social worker. Three things about her remain with me; she listened, was kind to me, and defended me. She tried to work with Loretta too and perhaps other members of my family, but I don't think it worked.

The best thing was when she said to me, "Pam, you're alright, they are not."

For many years, I treasured those words and the gift that she gave me, a blue, green and red enamel bracelet. It mattered. It was precious and reminded me that someone was on my side.

I am sure much more happened in our sessions and during our walks in Central Park but, "Pam you're alright," was what I so needed, and she gave it to me.

Life went along as usual. At about age twelve, I left junior high and moved onto high school. I had a best friend Bernice, who also came from Jamaica.

We took the same classes and coincidentally were always dressed alike. As I wasn't officially allowed to visit her or use the phone to talk to her, we had lunch together and used every opportunity to talk about anything and everything.

I know many young people didn't have the luxury of being able to use the telephone to talk to their friends, but I think many had friends outside of school, a sibling or a cousin to speak to, which I did not.

My Uncle Alfredo was always clear that schoolwork mattered, and he wanted to know about it. Fortunately, I still had the discipline developed in Jamaica of doing my homework. I don't remember much about what happened at high school as far as learning was concerned but it wasn't a problem.

During the summer holiday, I went to summer school. I enjoyed sports and became a decent volleyball player.

I also spent my time engrossed in reading every book in the house, many inappropriate for my age. This helped me escape into different worlds that I knew nothing about. I still remember the raciness of 'Lady Chatterley's Lover', the journey through 'Great Expectations' and 'Of Mice and Men.' I also read novels about slaves and their owners, which wasn't taught or even talked about in Jamaica.

My family continued to provide for me, doing the best within their understanding and capabilities. But really, they knew nothing about my world and the deep connection that I was yearning for inside.

# Falling in Love

At fourteen years old, I fell in love for the first time, as I saw it then. Delroy was a handsome young man from Jamaica, and he seemed kind of cool, with the neatest dreadlocks.

He was older than me, but I don't know how much, it never occurred to me to ask. I was too flattered that he was interested in me to ask any questions. I needed someone to like me. Also, because of my increased interest in all things Jamaican, (linked to my family's apparent rejection of our culture), I thought Delroy was perfect for me and our relationship developed further.

Being around Delroy brought me comfort as Jamaica was where I'd had positive experiences, except for the trauma of the beatings. We sometimes talked at the school gate and, on other occasions, I'd take the long way home and go to his flat.

We talked, kissed and had sex. Delroy was, as far as I was concerned, my boyfriend. I had no knowledge of contraception so, the risks we took were incredible.

One afternoon, after I had known him for a while, my friend Bernice and I worked out how we could spend time with him and his friends without our families knowing. He told us to meet him at his flat. When we got there, we were greeted with the sight of middle-aged women cooking in the kitchen. They didn't pay us any attention as we walked past the door.

I could hear the low sound of reggae music playing in the background. The whole place had the aroma of stewed chicken and rice and peas laced with coconut cream, which reminded me of Aunt Dar's delicious cooking.

The flat was of a poorer standard than the homes I had lived in. It was a bare and unloved environment, the type of home my family would not want me to visit. "Too rough," is what they'd say. But to me, it was intriguing.

Young men were coming and going while we waited. It was quite busy as we sat in the living room on the worn brown settee. A couple of guys came in and sat on another sofa and were talking to each other. Eventually, Delroy came home. He sat next to me and, after a little while, whispered, "Come with me."

Bernice was talking to one of his friends by then, so we left them to it and went into Delroy's bedroom. We sat on the bed talking and kissing, then after a short time he left me saying, "I'm coming right back."

After waiting for a few minutes, the door opened. I could see that the living room across the hallway was filled with more young men. Someone came into the bedroom. I expected it to be Delroy but as I looked up from where I was sitting on the bed, I saw that it was someone else.

The young man walked in, closed the door and sat next to me.

"Lie down!" he instructed in his Caribbean accent.

"Why?" I said, surprised. "What do you want? Where's Delroy?"

He ignored my questions.

"You no hear weh mi seh? Lie down!"

My heart began to pound, beating through my skin. He pushed me down from my sitting position on the bed, opened his trousers and proceeded to force himself on me. To rape me. He even wanted me to act like I was enjoying it.

*Oh no! What? Oh shit…* My mind raced in panic. *Where is Delroy? Does he know this is happening?*

I could not run. This was real danger. No escape was possible. *Oh my God!* I couldn't trigger the instinct to run and I was too scared to fight. In any case, after the beatings before, I had lost my ability to believe I could fight.

One by one, other men came into the room, some with different Caribbean accents.

*I've gone and done it this time,* I thought. *I'm really in danger now.*

Disgusted, disorientated and petrified, my only form of defence was to stiffen and close my legs tightly. I could hear from the muffled sounds coming from my friend in the next room that she was suffering the same horrendous experience. I heard them saying to her the same things that they said to me.

"Open yuh blood claart leg! Shut yuh mout!" one of them yelled as he pried open my legs.

I must have closed them even tighter for the last of five because I was so repulsed by his dirty appearance and ugly face. He was short, his dread-locks were clumpy, and they had a pungent smell to them. I didn't know at the time what that smell was. I later learned that it was marijuana.

As this one lay on top of me, my body was stiff with repulsion. His pride must have been hurt. He reached into the pocket of the jacket he was still wearing and took out a small gun. He rammed it into my side, shouting, "Open yuh fucking leg!"

I did so slowly, trembling with absolute terror. The appearance of the gun made me understand that I could lose my life. I had to go with what was happening.

I had no choice. Whilst he was enjoying himself, I was making sure I didn't show him my repulsion, so that I could live. I was in absolute fear but succumbed to survive.

The best way that I can describe how it felt is to say, I was totally mentally overwhelmed, fearing for my life, shocked and traumatised. I didn't want to feel anything, but I simultaneously felt pain and fatigue along with the physiological responses to sexual stimulation. It was mind-blowing. My mind paralysed but my body unable to be paralysed. A zombie!

Finally, after the fifth man, they stopped coming in. I started to put on my clothes and no one else entered. I knew it was over.

As I got up to leave, thoughts swam through my head.

*I will go home and never mention it. I will listen to my uncle from now on and always go straight home from school. I am never going to tell anyone about this. I will pretend it didn't happen. This must be why they said I should come straight home from school. Oh my God! It's my fault!*

I opened the door and slowly stepped out. I saw my friend coming out of the next room. She was in tears. I was so traumatised that I could not cry. There were now only a few young men in the living room and Delroy was nowhere in sight.

Bernice and I walked out past the kitchen where one of the older women was cleaning up. We made our way through the door and down the three flights of stairs until we found ourselves out in the fresh air. Then we headed to our different homes. When we parted, we didn't even speak. An all-consuming silence.

I went straight up to my room and to bed. I heard that ringing in my ears again, the same sound I heard in Jamaica when I was beaten. Just like the sound you hear when you have tinnitus. I understand now that this is a sign of trauma. I felt like I was being sucked down into quicksand and then slept deeply.

I don't know how long I was asleep before someone woke me to say that the police were here. I think it was my uncle.

*Oh my God, they know!* I thought.

I later discovered that my friend went home and told her father. I don't remember what happened next except that I went with the police. My friend and I both identified the flat. It was raided, and they were all eventually arrested.

Loretta called me every name under the sun. "You slut. You bitch…" she cried. "Look at the shame you have brought onto the family! Because of you, our name is in the newspaper. We've lived here for years and never had the police involved in our lives."

*Where will I find kindness?*

My older brother, Roberto. He was the only person who didn't make me feel worse. He accompanied and supported me during those days in court when while still petrified, I gave evidence about what happened to me.

The five men were found guilty of rape. They were all deported for this and the police discovered other things, including boxes of drugs under the floorboards. Delroy was deported for his drug dealing activities.

After the court case, I was in what seemed a permanent daze. I had to move in with my mother's friend for a little while, and then with Roberto and his wife and baby. I enjoyed living with my brother. He bought me a bike, but it got stolen, so I didn't learn to ride it properly.

A few months later, I was told that I was going to live with my father in England. Loretta had persuaded him to take me. My father to the rescue! I was certain I was going to something better now, a new start.

# England

I was fifteen when I arrived in London in July 1975. Another aeroplane trip to a strange country didn't bother me. I was used to it and wanted to leave the painful experiences behind.

I was happy to be going to my father, a real parent at last. I didn't know much about him, but I was sure he would help me. Loretta said it was time for him to finally take on his responsibility.

I will never forget the first time I met my father, Vernon. As I walked through the arrivals lane at the airport, two men walked towards me. I wanted the taller and younger of the two middle-aged men to be my father.

To my annoyance, it was the short one who came and planted a kiss. Not on my cheek or even my forehead, he actually kissed me on the lips!

The taller man, who as it turned out was my father's friend, took us home.

As we drove, I noticed that the roads, cars and buildings were smaller than they were in America. Also, the man speaking on the radio had a different accent.

We arrived where my father lived in Brixton, London. The house was smaller than the one in Brooklyn. We walked to the top floor where a woman opened the door. She looked just the way I remembered my Aunt Dar; grey hair, a round face and a pale brown complexion. A feeling of warmth and elation came over me when, in my confusion, I thought she was my great-aunt. The illusion of her being Aunt Dar lifted my spirits until she greeted me with a smirk.

"Hello," she muttered then turned her back. She was not friendly at all.

It turned out that she was my father's current wife, Daisy, the woman he had an affair with when he was married to my mother.

We had two rooms in the small house that was also rented to two other families. All three families shared the two bathrooms and a kitchen. This really was a different world!

During the winter, they had paraffin heaters to keep the place warm. I had never seen one before and once I even burnt my knees on it. This was a less affluent environment than I had experienced in Jamaica and Brooklyn.

Sometimes my father and I went to Brixton market. The smells that the food produced reminded me of Jamaica. The memories of Yallahs and Morant Bay markets came whooshing back. There were familiar fruits and vegetables like mangoes, plantains, bananas and some unfamiliar fruits too.

People were dressed less flamboyantly and in darker colours than in New York. The black people had a range of different accents, some were from the Caribbean and some from Africa. There were Indian, Chinese, and white people there too.

My father often made me laugh. He challenged me to races as we walked through the streets of London, the rule was that we had to avoid stepping on the cracks in the pavement. Whoever won, we both laughed heartily at the end of each race. If on these trips we found a coin, as we often did, he gave it to me.

We played cards in the evening, 'Rummy' or 'Remembrance', the game where you had to remember where the matching card was placed.

On our way to see his (usually female) friends, we hopped on or off buses. He had a free bus pass because of working for London Transport. He was happy to have me, his daughter, with him.

On the face of it, my father was a happy man who loved to talk. He regularly told me that he thought I looked like my mother. This was great to hear. At least I now knew something about her. He had a photograph of my mother with Loretta when she was a young child in Jamaica. This was the first time I saw what my mother, Rosita looked like. She wasn't exactly as I imagined but she was beautiful nonetheless.

I regularly inspected the picture and could see that I had similar features. My eyes were the same as my mother's, so were my lips and full cheeks. But my face was the shape of my father's.

My father told me that he loved Rosita, but she left him. He said lots of other things about her, he didn't understand boundaries. Vernon blurted everything out like, "She was going to abort you, but I stopped her."

Wow! Just what a child does not need to hear! It cemented my suspicion that my mother didn't want me. He had no thought about the impact on me. I was hurt yet so hungry to hear about her that I almost appreciated knowing this.

My father was angry with my mother for not wanting to come to England with him and for leaving him by going to America with her brother.

At last, here was an adult who talked to me. But he never spoke about the rape in New York or the beating in Jamaica.

He was angry with Aunt Dar who he said should never have sent me to New York. He didn't approve. "She should have kept you in Jamaica," he tutted. "You were meant to stay there until I came back to Jamaica so that you could look after me in my old age.

She sided with your mother and she shouldn't have done that. She is my aunt, my family, not your mother's."

It was the first time I heard about this family conflict and I didn't know how to respond. Despite this, at first, I was happy living with Vernon.

I slept in the same bedroom-cum-living room as him and my step-mother. They only had two rooms and my brother Oliver, who was already living with them, was in the other room. I slept on a single pull out bed right next to the side where Daisy slept.

One summer's night, about two months after I arrived, I woke up in the dark room to find my father sitting on my bed with his hand in my underwear.

"What are you doing?" I gasped.

"Shish," he whispered, with his face above mine. Those brown eyes with the blue circle looking back at me angrily, as though I had committed a crime. "You know you like it!" he smiled.

"Get off me," I shouted. I felt shocked, disappointed and betrayed all at the same time.

As he jumped up, Daisy, who was laying in the bed right next to mine, turned her head to look at what was going on. Then, she turned her back 'kissing her teeth' making that chirping sound.

My father then walked around to his side of the bed and laid down. They said nothing to each other or to me. He simply went back to sleep.

I was shocked, I lay there thinking about what just happened. Why didn't I get up, shout and make a big scene? Who would listen? Who cared? Where could I find rescue?

Not long after that occasion, I woke up to find him lying on top of me again, having sex with me, his fifteen-year-old daughter.

"Get off, leave me alone." When I tried to push him away, he stiffened, increasing the strength of his force.

He didn't stop, and after a while, I didn't fight him. I was already defeated. Like the time when I got raped by the men in New York. My fighting spirit weakened from the beatings in Jamaica.

It happened several times but when I finally spoke to him about it, his justification was that I had been having sex already. That was his reference to the rape. He told me to make sure I didn't mention it to anyone.

Later, I told him I'd tell on him. I didn't really know who I'd tell but I said it anyway. After that, he stopped having sex with me but was always looking for an opportunity to touch my breasts or my legs. It was a bizarre and risky existence living there.

In the September, I started attending a girls-only secondary school in Stockwell, Lambeth. This time I was the American girl that the Caribbean girls were fascinated by.

Oh, how America was a glorified place! There was no teasing. I was the novelty, they imagined that I was somehow more than they were because I had lived in the US.

I had one close friend who reminded me of Bernice who experienced the rape with me in Brooklyn. Even the girls (white and black) with whom I had a cursory relationship had a story that was similar to mine, living in situations where they were unhappy.

I did my best to adjust to a new education system in the UK. During the one year that I was in school, I obtained some Certificates of Secondary Education (CSEs). Social Studies was my favourite subject. I had a great teacher called Mrs Clark who believed in me. She was the first person I met when I joined the school. She asked me what I wanted to become, and I said, "a social worker." I was sure about that.

Mrs Clark had a face that was always smiling. There was never the need for her to shout, she just spoke. There were no hurdles to get over with her, she effortlessly connected with her pupils. Mrs Clark seemed to quietly, genuinely know what I needed. She may even have known what was going on in all our lives.

The main thing is that she was interested in me and I lived up to that. I was well mannered, presentable and focused, despite what was going on at home and I went on to become a prefect. My father supplied what I needed in terms of school uniform, clothes and a little bit of pocket money. He took this from the money Daisy gave back to him after he handed over his wages every Friday evening.

I always thought this was ludicrous, seeing him beg for a little more of the money he earned. Vernon couldn't handle money well. When he won at the betting shop, on his flutter on the horses or the dogs, he snuck some of that money to me as well, so I could buy sanitary towels and other things. I'm glad that I didn't have to ask my step-mother. How do you ask someone you don't know and who does not like you, for anything?

From the start, Daisy made it clear that I was not welcome. Our relationship started on the wrong foot really. Daisy didn't speak to me. She just told my father when dinner was ready, and he then asked me if I wanted to eat.

The one occasion she attempted to engage with me related to 'female things', but this conversation from someone who didn't usually talk to me was so incongruous that I didn't know how to respond. She told me that I should sit over a pail of warm water when my period ended, (a type of cleansing activity).

*What is this woman talking about? Why is she talking to me about this? I don't know her!*

When my father wasn't home, Daisy vented her anger at me, through her manner and her vicious words. If she decided to sweep the living room, she did so aggressively, causing me to get up and go sit on the stairs.

If she was cooking and I was in earshot, she said things like, "She tink she better than me, 'bout she nuh eat yam or green banana."

She was angry with me for lots of reasons; my mother, my father having sex with me, my whole existence. It didn't help that my father regularly told her that he loved my mother and had only married her on the advice of his Pastor because she had Oliver for him.

Although I was hungry to hear the stories about his life with Rosita, it didn't make Daisy feel good at all.

For my part, I was in an uncomfortable dilemma. I wanted him to tell me about my mother and I didn't like Daisy but knew he was wrong to ignore her feelings. And all the while I was trying to forget his sexual abuse of me.

It was in October, a few months after my arrival in the UK, when I first saw Fitz. One evening, I was looking out the window, when I noticed him walk past my gate.

*He's good looking!* I thought.

This went on for a few evenings with me pulling the curtain to one side and watching him. Eventually, he looked up and smiled. Sometimes, I'd make sure I was outside putting the rubbish in the bin precisely at the moment he walked by. On a few occasions, he stopped, and we chatted briefly. Finally, we arranged to meet.

Our first date was just a walk, in a nearby park, where we sat and talked for a while. He asked me about America and I told him about the enormous buildings and roads and how affluent things were. I asked him about his life. He told me he lived alone and worked in the Post Office. We decided we liked each other and our relationship continued from there. Fitz sometimes picked me up from school in his car. We usually went for a drive before he dropped me at the end of the road, so I could walk home. This was to prevent my father seeing us.

One evening after school, when we were sitting in his car, I told Fitz more about my life. Some of the unpleasant aspects but not all. I didn't tell him about the rape, because I couldn't talk about it at that time. But I told him about the beatings and said my father was a pervert. Fitz listened carefully, he didn't say much except from time to time, "Tell me more."

Feeling ashamed, I eventually said what Vernon had done to me. Fitz responded by shaking his head from side to side. He didn't say anything, but I think after this he wasn't afraid of Vernon finding out about us. He knew something about him that he could fight back with.

Fitz told me some things about his life as well. "My mother left me in Jamaica too. I was sixteen when she sent for me after leaving me for ten years. I came up on a scholarship. Do you know the first thing that woman said to me when I arrived?"

"No, what?" I asked.

"She said, you better go to work and give me back the plane fare!"

After this conversation, I started to develop a deep bond with Fitz, which lasted twenty years. This was mainly due to my need for protection, for a rescuer and my mistaken belief that gratefulness was love. It felt like a definition of love to me. For his part, he was proud that he had landed a good-looking young girl. He was the envy of his friends.

Fitz was thirteen years older than me, but the age gap didn't bother me. He became a buffer from my father's abuse. My only criterion was that he liked me and was on my side, he was someone who could and would, defend me, or so I imagined. I made him into my saviour, his existence was enough for me to use as a shield. I felt safer.

I never considered whether he would make a good husband, father or breadwinner. Those things did not occur to me. I was only fifteen. Who thinks of this at that age? I knew he was handsome, slim and from Jamaica. That was enough for me. Fitz was a man who, underneath his confident exterior, didn't have much self-belief.

He loved science. He read books about chemistry and physics and he did mathematics equations every spare minute he got. Yet, his low self-esteem left him believing he could do nothing with his intelligence.

Fitz believed and regularly said, "The white man won't let me…" become this or that. This was his ingrained belief because of what he saw and experienced. He felt disempowered.

For my part, I never believed I wasn't good enough to be whatever I wanted to be. I had no concept that anyone could stop me, so I felt all he had to do was try. I thought he only needed help and I was going to repay him for rescuing me and being my protector by doing just that.

My father found out about us when he saw me with Fitz one day. I didn't know he had seen us and when I got home, he screamed at me. "You think I didn't see you with that man? You better not see him again."

I didn't say anything to his rantings.

After this, I thought my father had guessed that Fitz knew what he had done to me. The idea that Fitz might know may have helped to keep my father away from me as thereafter he stopped trying to touch me.

Then one day when Daisy wasn't at home, Vernon returned from work and saw me sitting on the settee. After eating his dinner, at the small dining table in the corner he pulled out a chair for me and said, "Come here a minute Pam."

I got up, and went to sit with him, wondering what now?

He looked at me and said in a conspiratorial tone, "Did you know that man you are seeing is married? He even has children," he muttered. "Disgusting, messing around with you, he has a wife!"

I didn't know what to say, I was shocked and hurt but also suspicious that he was trying to split us up.

The next day when Fitz came to pick me up from school, I told him what Vernon said and asked if it was true. Fitz admitted to having children but denied being married and told me his children's mother treated him badly and they were sleeping in separate rooms. I believed him because I needed to, and from then on, my empathy for Fitz deepened. He was poorly treated by the mother of his children and by his own mother. My father had lied about him and was trying to split us up.

Together we bonded against the cruelty and unfairness of our parents and the other people in our lives. Fitz was protecting me from Vernon, and I was going to make his life better.

This was our unspoken deal. I had no sense that Fitz was exploiting my vulnerability. We were in this together. We agreed that Vernon was trying to stop me seeing him, so he could continue to molest me. Our bond grew closer. We were united against the world.

Many years later, Fitz told me that my father once paid him to stop seeing me. So, Fitz took the money but carried on seeing me!

# Adulthood

Fitz and I had been together almost nine months by the time I finished school aged sixteen, in the summer of 1976. By then we, my father Vernon, Daisy, Oliver and I had moved into a new flat in Lambeth.

One evening, I left the flat with my party clothes and shoes in a bag saying I was going to see a friend, the thing a lot of us did when we weren't allowed to go to out partying.

I walked down the road to where Fitz picked me up in his car. We drove to the Bouncing Ball Club in Peckham where there was a dance night going on.

These dances were popular in the 1970's, the era when reggae music made its way to the UK and even onto British TV. The Bouncing Ball and the Bali Hai Club in Streatham were not to be missed on a Saturday night, certainly not by me.

These were places where the DJs re-created memories of Jamaica and the Caribbean with the sounds bellowing out of giant speakers.

The rhythm of the music bound couples tightly together until the early morning dawn. Finding a source of joy and connection with our home countries. Easing the pressure for some, making it possible to continue in the hostile climate of 1970's London. In this intoxicating environment, I momentarily lost all fear of the consequences of being out so late. That was until Fitz said it was time to go home.

Fitz dropped me off, and while I walked up the stairs to our flat, I wondered what I'd say if I was asked. There was a part of me that didn't really care,

*What was the worst that they could do?*

With my father knowing I had some kind of protection from Fitz, I figured he couldn't and wouldn't hit me or do anything about it.

I put my key in the lock and turned it. But the door didn't open.

*Oh hell, what is up with these damn people? I am tired, I want to go to bed. There is no chance of me sneaking back in!*

So, I knocked hard enough to wake them up.

In the past when this happened, Daisy opened the door and moaned or 'kissed her teeth', and I'd make my way to my bedroom regardless of her attitude.

On this occasion, both my step-mother and my father stood at the slightly ajar door blocking my entrance.

"I know you went out with Fitz," Vernon yelled. "Go back to him."

It seemed simple to me. "Fine," I said and left.

I am not sure they expected that response! I am not sure where it even came from. I was just weary, I guess, tired of the nonsense that was my life with them. That was the last time I saw my father and his wife for 13 years. I never went back to live there. My only regret was that I left my mother's candlestick shaped perfume bottle there. How I wish I still had it.

Fitz had already left, and I couldn't go to his house because he was living with his children and his 'not' wife.

I walked to where a friend from school lived nearby. She had a baby while at school and, as fate would have it, had just moved into a flat. I went to stay with her for a few days, sleeping on her new carpet while she was waiting for furniture to arrive.

In my purse, I had the address of a friend of my brother, Oliver, who knew me from Jamaica. She had visited my father's house a few days before I left, looking for my brother. She left her address for me to give to him. I decided to go and see her with the intention of asking if I could stay with her.

I took a bus from Brixton in South West London and headed for New Cross in the South East. As luck would have it, she lived in a purpose-built house. It was the type of accommodation that students live in now, with ten rooms with a single bed, wardrobe and a sink, a large shared kitchen and bathrooms.

A room next to hers was empty. We forced the door open and that is where I squatted for four months until the Housing Association realised I was there. After I pleaded with them, they allowed me to stay on, paying rent. Fitz helped out, with food and money, and I became friends with another young woman in the room on the opposite side.

I survived the years after being asked to leave my father's home, driven by the desire to fulfil my dreams. I never forgot the job I wanted to do; becoming a social worker who listened to children, just like my social worker did for me in New York. I never forgot my mission. I had the confidence my Aunt Dar planted in me, that I could achieve whatever I wanted. I knew I wanted to give young girls a voice, the voice I didn't have back then.

There were some things I understood and wanted to use to help. I had a sense of why girls could be raped, sexually exploited and abused. I knew that the key or trigger for abusers is the whiff of vulnerability that they carry, just as I had at that age.

Because of my experiences, I instinctively knew that strengthening children by addressing emotional deficits is the key to their survival. I realised that children and young people needed other people to look out for them. They needed a community of adults to act for them.

This is what my difficult experiences had led me to understand. The only thing was, these experiences were a secret known only to me, Fitz and a few trusted others. In my view, it was unsafe to share it widely.

I was convinced that there would be judgement about what happened to me. The critic in me kept blaming me, the child, for what others had done and then feeling bad about being a vulnerable child.

I decided that I'd achieve my ambition by hook or by crook. My father's insistence on me learning the type of things a secretary knows was a valuable gift from him. He was clear that being a secretary was the best job for me, a woman. He was not aware of a job called social worker or my intention to become one. When, in secondary school, I took a class called Commerce which included typing, I didn't realise that the career I chose would eventually need this skill so much. I thought social work needed skills to work with children and parents to cause change. I probably wouldn't have chosen it if I knew most of my time would have to be spent typing into a computer, the way it is now!

As it happened, typing helped me to earn a living until I achieved my ambition. Commerce had other advantages too, it was helpful for my initial understanding of business. Who knew that I'd make use of this introduction and expand my knowledge of business to the extent I have now?

After leaving home, sheer determination resulted in me getting jobs. My friend and neighbour, June and I worked out a way to extend our individual wardrobes. We wore, washed and exchanged our clothes.

The day I got my very first job, I was on a mission. I got dressed and took the bus to Oxford Street. I walked along Oxford Street and asked in every shop for a job.

I eventually got my first job in Barratt's shoe shop, which was next to Selfridges at the time. The supervisor was a great trainer, and I did very well getting customers to buy shoes, especially Arab women who bought lots of them at the same time. After that, I got another job in a stationary company in Old Street, as a 'Girl Friday.' I wanted a better job because I knew I could do better and I needed more money. I went to an agency and took a typing test then obtained another position in a typing pool, supporting the secretary of a senior person in an American company in Victoria Street, London.

I eventually became the company cashier, checking their bank accounts in different currencies, handing out petty cash, paying expense claims and other accounting jobs in the firm.

During this time, I was in communication with Aunt Dar. Since I arrived in England, she had started writing and I shared some aspects of my life with her, but nothing explicit, especially when it came to my father. She knew I wasn't living with him and that his wife was not kind to me.

I was saving the detail for when I went home to Jamaica again to tell her. I wanted to see her. She was, essentially, my mother. It was the place where, but for the beating, I received the best treatment.

After I left his house, the only thing I heard about my father was in letters from my great-aunt. She told me about something he did, the injustice of which stings even now.

Vernon and Daisy had gone to Jamaica on holiday but were frightened that I may have told Aunt Dar about his sexual abuse of me and that she told others.

So, they spread a lie that I had become pregnant by a married man and had to have an abortion. They planted that seed about me because abortions were considered immoral. So now I was a thief, a liar and immoral!

By then Aunt Dar had become my arch defender and wrote to tell me of my father's actions and her intention to disinherit him as a result.

I was determined to go on holiday to see her. To be able to feel a mother's love again and to understand the beating, to know exactly why it happened. To achieve this, I worked every morning from 5:30 am. doing an office cleaning job before freshening up dressing again and moving on to my day job which was not too far away. Sometimes I'd do an evening cleaning job too.

Eventually, I had enough money to go home to Jamaica. It felt important for me to go and see Aunt Dar, to lay my head on her ample breast for the comfort I needed, like I did as a very young child.

# Going Home

I was eighteen when I returned to Jamaica on holiday. Aunt Dar met me at the airport and we hugged each other. The joy of seeing her was almost absolute, apart from the internal sadness and confusion about what she had done to me.

Oh, the joy of seeing my home again after years of living in two foreign countries with people who had been strangers to me, including my family!

I tried to pretend that I didn't still feel ashamed and embarrassed that others may have believed negative things about me including that I took the money that she had wrongly and so publicly accused me of stealing.

As soon as we got to her house, Aunt Dar fussed over me. "Pam, look," she said, as she uncovered a table full of my favourite things. "Look what I have for you."

The dining table had a gizzada pie full of grated coconut with ginger, nutmeg and cinnamon, along with coconut drops and a cake she baked.

The smell of rice and peas and chicken, like only Aunt Dar could cook it, was invigorating. The wonderful aspects of my childhood memories came gushing back. I was in the warm arms of love. I didn't know where to start and when to stop. She sat at the table looking at me as I ate, filling the hole that had been left in me when I left her.

The next day, Aunt Dar invited me into her bedroom where she proudly showed me the trunk full of the nightgowns, housecoats, sheet sets and underwear I had sent her over the years. She was saving them all up for when she might have to go to hospital, after all, you had to look your best in hospital!

Her role in helping others was still apparent. The things that weren't in the trunk had been given away to her friends or to people who needed them more than she did.

A few years before, Aunt Dar had remarried, to someone younger than herself. The man was the local builder who told me he was grateful she accepted his proposal. He was very respectful to her when I was there, but other people told me he had a reputation for womanising and for owing money around the district.

My great-aunt still had young girls living with her, because their families couldn't look after them well; The impact of poverty. I got along well with one of the girls. She talked to me about both Aunt Dar's kindness and her bouts of cruelty. These were always linked to her stress, particularly when her new husband had done something disrespectful to her.

I helped the girls by listening and giving them strategies to cope, including making them aware that their families could be enlisted to help on these occasions. They needed to know that they didn't have to put up with Aunt Dar's ill-treatment. One of them heeded my advice and left, despite the worry about not having as good a life as she was having with my great-aunt. She went to live with her own aunt but eventually went back to help Aunt Dar, who by then was an old lady who had become increasingly frail and more cautious. She knew that this young woman on whom she depended, would leave her again if she continued to mistreat her.

Overall, I loved being home again. I climbed my mango trees, the trees that I'd nurtured as a child. I ate the fruits from them, I preferred the fruit from my East Indian mango tree, but the Julie mangoes were good too.

My great-aunt and I got great joy from being back together. I reconnected with my yard, my community and my country. I even hooked up with a boy who was one of my next-door neighbours, someone I liked as a child and who used to smile at me. When he came over in the evenings he greeted Aunt Dar respectfully as she sat in her usual spot on the veranda.

"Good evening Aunt Dar."

"Good evening Trevor," she replied with authority. Then they'd exchange pleasantries as she asked after his mother and had a few moments of small talk. After a little while, he asked if he could speak with me and, after a pause, she called me.

When I came out to sit with Trevor, Aunt Dar stayed firmly in her spot on the veranda.

One day as we were talking, subtly flirting, she called me over to her side of the veranda and beckoned me to come closer for her to whisper in my ear.

"You see how him teeth kin? It's the same way his great-uncle used to come to Orange Park, come kin him teeth with me every evening. You can't trust them."

She meant that the two men had similarities in their courting approach and they weren't to be believed. A warning of sorts. I found her intervention hilarious, mainly because I had already decided that I was interested in this young man and found a way to meet up with him without her there.

When I went for a walk in the evenings, Trevor and I usually met by the beach where we sat and had a great time reminiscing about things that happened when we were younger.

The best thing about being back in Jamaica was that it was the place where my mother had lived. People who knew her, random strangers recognised that I was her child.

"Pam, you're Miss Rosita's baby, aren't you?" the older people called out as I passed them in the street.

"I remember you, the skinny foot pickney!"

"Oh, Miss Rosita!"

It was interesting to hear people declare my mother's name with warmth and love. I didn't think I could ask them about her. How embarrassing to ask strangers to tell me about my own mother!

They told me I used to be crying at her feet as she worked in her shop. I wanted her to pick me up, but she didn't, according to them.

*This is more evidence that she didn't want me,* I thought. *She didn't even pick me up when I was crying.*

Interestingly, I didn't ask Aunt Dar about my mother either. I think I was scared she would repeat my father's story about her not wanting me. But just before leaving, I summoned up enough courage to do one of the things I went to Jamaica to do.

I was prompted by a school friend who passed the yard and called out to me, "Pam, did you really come back to see that cruel woman after what she did to you?"

*I knew it,* I thought. *People remembered what happened.* At the time, I was sure they believed I was a thief.

So, a few days before I was to return to the UK, as we sat close together on the veranda, I finally asked, "Aunt Dar, why did you accuse me of taking that money and then beat me so badly, when I didn't do it?"

She looked at me and said, "Pam, I don't remember that."

"How could you forget that?" I gasped.

"I don't remember," she whispered and spoke no more. Her lips closed tightly, looking straight ahead. What an awkward interaction.

The lady, who had so much to say before, didn't have anything to say about this. I was disappointed, speechless and hurt, almost as much as when she accused and beat me. She did this incredible thing again. She lied.

So, I never discovered the reason my Aunt Dar accused me of taking money, then beat me and paraded me around for all to see and believe I was a thief.

I can only think that she wanted to be able to get more money from my father. If it was stolen by me and everyone he asked in the local area could confirm it, he couldn't accuse her of taking his money.

Over the subsequent years when I visited Jamaica, I heard gossip about the money being given to Colin, her handyman, to buy a new motorbike.

*Was this true? I don't know if together they made up the story. Did they conspire to accuse me, so my father would send some more money? Did Colin have something on her? Was he in a relationship with her that he threatened to tell others about and that might have embarrassed her, given her status? Had she just misplaced the money and found it?*

I will never know, she died never telling me the truth.

I have seen Colin in recent years when I've returned to Jamaica. Previously, not understanding his role but wanting a connection with my past, I used to bring him a shirt, a pair of shoes and even take his order for the next time. There must have been a reason for his permanent inability to look me in the eye. I plan to sit him down the next time I am in Jamaica and ask him to tell me the truth. Perhaps he will want to before he dies.

It's hard to accept the idea that they could have conspired to publicly brand me a thief to cover their actions. But re-reading the letters my aunt wrote to my father at the time, of the incident, I see it's likely that some sort of 'plot' was the reason for the brutal public assault that I endured.

I don't know if Aunt Dar believed I took the money at any stage, but I do know that she descended into madness. The days of beatings felt like she was taking out all her anger about her life on me.

Aunt Dar was angry about her reduced financial circumstances, the lowering of her status, the adultery of both her husbands and the burden of responsibility of raising me. Nothing was working for her.

The abuse I received reminded me of the films I see of slaves, who through beatings and humiliation are broken. Some become angry, some more determined than ever to get free. It is the same utter madness that still occurs, not just in my culture but in many others. Perhaps not always so extreme but having the same terrible impact nonetheless.

In my case, I became more determined than ever to become a social worker, to help children who had gone through similar experiences.

# Reconnecting

In September 1978, I came back to the UK, which by now seemed more like home than Jamaica because Jamaica wasn't a place where I found truth.

I went back to my job and did one or two evening classes every year for five years, ending up with the necessary qualifications I needed to study to become a social worker.

I found out that I could volunteer in the evenings and at weekends, befriending young people in the criminal justice system and in care.

Working with trained youth workers, I helped conduct the group work sessions and sometimes we went on trips to help the young people to feel better. We guided them through some of their difficulties.

I was allocated one set of siblings who needed a positive association with someone from their parental racial background, especially as they had been placed away from their community. Two of us spent time talking to them and going to museums or playing games. We got to know them, they told us a lot of things about themselves during our time together. They were lovely young people, they needed positive role models and I took great pleasure in helping them.

Meanwhile, I met many people in my day job as a cashier. There was a young man, who was training to become an accountant. We often went to lunch and even spent a weekend together once. There was much to commend him to me. His father was a diplomat and he talked about us having a life together. This man may have been a more suitable option for me than Fitz, he was certainly closer to my age. But I couldn't choose him over Fitz.

I also met another young man whom I adored, exactly my type, with the beautiful complexion of my Uncle John. He was studying law and told me how proud he was of me for managing on my own without a family, going to night-school, learning to drive and pursuing my career. This time I seriously considered leaving Fitz and marrying him, even without anything happening between us.

We didn't get very far though because, when he asked me to make a commitment to leave Fitz in order to have a relationship with him, I backed out. We were supposed to meet up after I had broken it off with Fitz, but I couldn't do it. I didn't turn up. I didn't see him again after that. I still often fantasise about this man.

*What is he doing now? Did he pass his exams to become a barrister? Did I make a mistake in not turning up?*

So why didn't I meet him? Deep down, I thought Fitz was what I deserved. I thought this other man was too good for me.

*What might he say if he knew about me? He wouldn't want me then. Would he?*

Fitz knew everything about me by now, and he stuck with me. We were inextricably bonded by shame. I believed there was no way another man would want me if he knew about my life, if he knew that I was 'unclean'. Such was my judgement of myself and my belief that others condemned me likewise.

In 1981, at the age of twenty-one, I met up with my Uncle Alfredo, whose house I had lived in Brooklyn. He was doing a tour of Europe.

The evening before I received a telephone call.

"Hello is this Pam? This is Uncle Alfredo, how are you?"

"Uncle Alfredo?

"Yes Pam. I'm in London. Where are you?"

My heart was pounding, I was bewildered and anxious that he was coming to see me, and I wasn't ready for it. Panicked I held my nerve, hoping he wasn't nearby.

"In New Cross, do you know where that is?"

"No, I am leaving in a couple days. Can we meet?"

"Yes, Uncle Alfredo?

"Do you know where Big Ben is?"

"Yes, I work about five minutes' walk from there."

"Meet me at 12:30 pm. tomorrow. Can you get a break from work to spend the afternoon with me?"

"Yes, Uncle Alfredo."

I put the phone down excited, anxious and tearful.

*He is speaking to me! He wants to see me after the shame I brought to him when I was raped!*

The next day when we met, the nervous bewildered 'child Pam' emerged. He took me shopping and bought me a gold necklace. This visit meant a reconnection with my family in America. After this, I arranged to visit them in New York.

Going back to America that first time was strange and I was afraid. I didn't feel safe, I was worried about whether the friends of the boys who raped me were still around.

I didn't know how Loretta felt about me. After all I was the one who she said had brought disgrace to the family.

When she and her husband Clay met me at the airport, I felt a range of emotions. I was happy to see them yet ashamed of getting raped, which I knew Loretta believed I had caused. I felt that they thought of me as a bad person, but I was unable to do anything about these thoughts and feelings. All these emotions came at once.

During my stay with them in Queens where they lived, Loretta and Clay took me out to shows and generally looked after me. Their daughter Natasha was a vivacious little girl. Her father, in particular, doted on her. He spent a lot of time with her, teaching her how to say and do things, laughing when she got it right. He was creating a miniature version of himself. Whenever he came home, my niece lit up, just like I did with my Uncle John when I was a child.

"Clay, you'll be sorry. Put her down, it's too much," Loretta said but Clay just carried on regardless.

Loretta made sure she noticed everything about Natasha and took proactive action. She wanted the very best for her daughter. Loretta wanted her to learn to dance, was interested in how she learned, her weight, everything a good mother cared about.

Loretta appeared to be the practical one of the two parents, steering her household. She was also still a mother figure to us, her siblings. Her home was the place everyone gravitated to and she was the leader who was asked for advice all the time. By now, she was also a senior nurse in charge of her ward in the hospital where she worked.

She was okay in relating to me, but I was still afraid, re-experiencing the feelings I'd had around her as a teenager. I even regressed, looking up to her for some sort of approval. It never came, but at least I didn't feel she was angry with me, like I did when I lived with them in Brooklyn.

But sister-mother and I still didn't really talk about anything significant. One day as we sat at the dining table, she asked me about my job. Just before I left for New York, someone at work had asked me if I wanted to be an international courier delivering packages for a well-known UK company. I told Loretta about this and she told me to be cautious, indicating that she cared about me, something I was still struggling to believe.

Loretta told me that our father had been to visit her recently and she was angry with him because he did a stupid thing. Not having seen her since she was a young child in Jamaica, he visited the United States and contacted her. She allowed him to visit her home and he was introduced to her husband's parents. To her dismay, not prompted by anything that was being said, Vernon embarked on a conversation about our mother that was so negative it embarrassed Loretta. This hurt her deeply as she had not chosen to divulge information about her mother or her life to her in-laws. Loretta said she was glad to see the back of him and she didn't intend to make contact with him in the future.

When I was due to leave, Loretta, Clay and Natasha took me to the airport. When I got there, I couldn't believe what I had done. I misread the departure time, we arrived too late, and I missed my flight! I felt so stupid. There I was, showing them how grown up I had become, and then I did this! I felt I had given them another reason to think badly of me. They were fine about it and I pledged to pay them back the airfare they had to cover. I paid them back as soon as I was able to save up enough money. I didn't want to owe them anything.

After this trip, Loretta and I wrote to each other and occasionally talked on the phone, not about much but certainly, more than we ever did. I told her about my job, but nothing else. She was like a distant mother, checking in on her daughter from time to time.

Not long after, Veronica, who by now was in the American Army, telephoned to say she was stationed in Germany and could come to see me in London for the weekend. This was a wonderful thing for me. I was excited about the visit. Veronica and I didn't talk about my time in New York.

Fitz saw that I had family and finally met one of my sisters. When Veronica and I chatted I told her some positive things about him like how he cooked delicious Jamaican food for me when I got home from work and about how intelligent he was. Veronica told me about her army life and gave me some pictures of herself.

A year later, when Veronica completed her time in the army and returned to New York, I visited Loretta again but this time it felt like I was going home. Loretta had not long had another baby girl, named Shakira.

Before I arrived, Veronica told me that Loretta was unwell. When I got there, it was clear to see that she was seriously ill but was still trying to manage. She had cancer, the type our mother had.

After I'd returned to the UK, I was told Loretta had deteriorated and was in hospital. Loretta died leaving behind her two beautiful little girls and her husband Clay. I arrived back in Brooklyn just after she was buried because, by the time I heard about her funeral, it was too late for me to get there.

Sitting with the two little girls, I was reminded that I didn't have a mother, just like them. I have stayed closely in touch with them to this day, loving them the way I wanted to be loved.

Not long after Loretta died, Clay asked me if I'd take Natasha because he had remarried and was struggling with her behaviour. He appeared to have no understanding that Natasha's behaviour could have been a reaction to the loss of and apparent replacement of her mother. He too was suffering because of loss and had done what he thought was best. But I couldn't help him even if I wanted to. At age twenty-one, I was struggling to survive in England.

Furthermore, I did not agree with this approach. I didn't think that they should have sent me away to England when I needed them most after the rape. I was not going to be complicit in a typical repeat of this unkind act. So, I refused, but Clay sent Natasha away anyway. As before when my mother died, my family like many others didn't believe or perhaps didn't know that therapy could help children with grief or that behaviours are the reasonable manifestation of feelings.

To this day, Natasha is affected by his decision. I hope she will be able to recover and get the support she needs, and that Natasha and Clay will one day rebuild their relationship. I hope we can become a talking family at last.

# Vernon

Although I didn't make contact with my father throughout this time, I found out more about his own story, also full of struggles.

Vernon was orphaned at a young age, which was common during the early 1940's in Jamaica. People died much earlier than people do today, and he was unfortunate to lose both of his parents within a couple of years of each other.

He once told me that he regularly moved to live with different relatives and because his complexion was much darker than other family members, he was treated as though he was less than them. They thought he was only good enough to help around the yard or do manual jobs.

He wasn't sent to school consistently, a fact that he thought was unfair and was bitter about. He had no opportunity to have a sustained education, although, he could read and write, as he had been educated up to primary school level. His handwriting was beautiful. He had perfected this in his spare time.

My father kept a card he once received that called him Dr Vernon Rowe. He was proud of being given this accolade because it fed his yearning for recognition.

This simple card was so important to him. I still have it now.

Vernon had all the other behaviours of someone from a middle-class family. He knew how to dress, had good manners and he was a guardian of etiquette. Even though his job was cleaning buses, he wore bespoke tailored suits from the world-renowned Saville Row. Never shy to wear a white suit, white shoes and accessorise with a pink handkerchief and tie, he was always immaculate. He knew how to conduct himself in public, and he had all the social graces; opening doors for women, offering his seat to someone less able and dining etiquette, including knowing the appropriate way to use cutlery. In other words he was a classy guy.

He was also a regular figure at weddings. I have seen him in countless wedding pictures. He was almost always the Master of Ceremonies due to his 'gift of the gab', which rendered him a confident, entertaining public speaker. A cousin recently told me that his uncle was at a wedding where my father said he had only just begun speaking, two hours after starting his speech!

Vernon had high standards about how people should conduct themselves and was obsessed about good timekeeping. He got very upset if anyone was late. I used to tell him to calm down as I didn't want him to have a heart attack.

Women loved Vernon. In Jamaica on holiday while I was visiting Miss Sonia, the lady I stayed with as a child, I overheard her and her friends, talking about when he lived in Jamaica.

Shaking her head and sighing deeply, one of the women said, "Vernon neva deserve the way Rosita treat him. Him should a neva married ar. She just go America wid ar bredda instead a wait fi him fi send fi ar?"

Miss Sonia said, "You see if him did marry me like him did promise, I would a look after him so till..."

Another declared, "Me neva figet when me madda did sick and me neva av de money fi pay de fare fi go a hospital. Dat man 'ear bout it and ride 'im bicycle fi miles fi bring it come gimme."

His small network of male friends tolerated him mainly because of his family history. After all, he was from the family who, back in Jamaica, gave them work or money when they needed to feed their families.

My cousins, his nieces and nephew, loved him partly because when his sister, their mother, died, he looked after them, helping to bring them up and to provide for them. This was one of his strengths.

He hadn't taken financial care of his own children but had immense compassion for children who were left parentless as he had been. His thinking was, at least his children had their parents. Having parents was his barometer for what children needed. He couldn't think further than that because of his experience of not having any himself.

Vernon, frequently told me the reason he loved my mother so much, was that she was the only one who went to visit his sister in hospital when she was dying of cancer. He said he decided to marry my mother because of this and because of her quick-wittedness. I soaked up every story he had to tell about my mother, good and bad. I was so desperate to know about her, to have a connection with her.

Of course, what I really wanted to know was why she left me and if she loved me. I could never ask though.

*What if the answer was no, as my father had indicated by telling me she wanted an abortion? What if she didn't want me even after I was born?*

There was a story he told me repeatedly. "Pam," he said, "One evening, me and your mother was heading home after going for a walk. She was looking pretty as ever, the most beautiful girl in the district. I was pushing my bicycle walking beside her, proud like a peacock." He grinned and sat up straight, reliving and savouring the memory, whilst I imagined the two of them together.

"My chest was high, I knew every man was jealous. Just as we stepped off the bridge, a man rode by. Guess what he had the audacity to say?

He shouted out, looking at your mother, 'You want a tow?' Well, quick as a flash, Rosita said, 'Me have ten already!"

My father explained that she meant she had the owner of ten toes beside her already, she had her man. This bowled Vernon over, and every time he told this story he laughed. It made me proud to have a quick-witted mother like that too.

According to him, my mother was also quick-tempered. He showed me a mark on his head made by a stone she threw at him when he came home late one evening after visiting his girlfriend, now my step-mother. He said my mother almost killed him, but he loved her nonetheless.

Vernon was not mentally very stable. He could occasionally become paranoid when emotionally affected by significant events. He told me about two occasions which he remembered vividly. He said he had a nervous breakdown after his sister died and she appeared and spoke to him. I think this went untreated. In Jamaica, there was no such luxury as a mental health service, of the kind we know in the UK.

Another time was when he received a letter from my mother asking him for a divorce, some years before she died. In his distress, he had gone to the market area of Brixton in London and started preaching incoherently. One of Uncle John's sons was living with him then and got him admitted to a psychiatric hospital. My father never forgave him for that.

When I look back at Vernon's life, I wonder about the impact of trauma on him. Was there anyone to teach him anything about morals or how to curtail his perversions? Left to bring himself up without any consistent parenting, he couldn't separate in his mind the fact that his daughter was not his wife.

*Was he just perverted? Was he molested? Did he see young daughters being molested and think it was normal? Was I the only child he had sex with?* I do not know, but I strongly suspect not.

His son Oliver was passively aggressive towards Vernon, perhaps because he was left, in his childhood, to grow up in Jamaica without his father and without much of anything. He saw how his mother struggled, and he didn't like the way our father treated her.

I think he thought that our father had more money than he did and deliberately chose not to help him and his mother. Or that Vernon didn't love him because he ignored him in the many years before he was brought to the UK as a teenager.

He heard how our father spoke about my mother. I also overheard Daisy sharing her feelings about this with Oliver. He once told me that our father supported my sister and I in the past. This wasn't true, but you can develop fantasies when no one tells you anything, when you don't have the facts.

Vernon regularly cursed Oliver for how he dressed and was anxious about whether he was securing a livelihood for himself. Oliver was the opposite of my father. He didn't care about appearances. He was happy to wear clothes with holes in them and that were creased and not ironed. He didn't cream his skin and he was never going to wear a suit. He is, in fact, a lifelong non-conformist, rebelling against our father.

# Daisy

My father's wife Daisy was an intriguing woman. She had the potential to love deeply. I saw this from the love that oozed out of her pores for Oliver. She also had the capacity to hate deeply, an aspect of her character that she reserved especially for me.

I will never forget the time that my father was out of the house and Daisy walked past my bedroom door as I lay on the bed reading. She paused for a minute and sneered, "You madda tek me man from me. you na go do de same ting!" I was shocked and didn't know what to say or do. In dismay, with tears running down my face, I turned my head to look at her as she walked on after delivering her warning.

I later discovered that Vernon had met Daisy at the same time as my mother and chose to marry my mother but continued his affair with Daisy.

It is possible she really didn't think my father's sexual abuse of me was a big deal, such was the prevalence of this kind of behaviour in her surroundings. Or perhaps the same thing had happened to her as well.

I say this because of what some of my friends tell me about their mother's lives in Jamaica and elsewhere. It seems that fathers raping their daughters was a common occurrence at that time. I know it's not that different now in Jamaica or anywhere else.

Daisy needed to stay with my father no matter what. She was caught up in the sanctity and security of marriage and the lack of other options.

My stepmother had struggled to bring up her siblings after their parents died. She was desperate never to be in a situation again where she didn't have food. To this day, her brothers love her for what she did for them.

Daisy continued to have a relationship with Vernon while he was with my mother, for reasons of survival. Here was a man from a 'good' family, considered 'rich' and educated. She had a child by him and had set her sights on getting this man for herself one day. Resolute, I understand she waited for over twenty years, except for the occasion when she had an affair with and got pregnant by the man whose house she was cleaning. Daisy bore a son called Frank, who the man's wife took in and looked after. Daisy hoped and prayed that my father would choose her one day and rescue her from her plight. He eventually did, many years later after my mother died.

Daisy had come to England in 1973, two years before I arrived. She was by far the better financial planner of the two, and she worked and controlled the money. She was determined to return to Jamaica and every day did something towards achieving her goal. She was a woman on a mission. Every week she bought something that was then stored in a corner of the flat for when she went back home. Daisy's life was a testament to what you can achieve if you are determined.

On the other hand, my father was too enamoured by having the opportunity to come to the UK. He did not want to leave at all, which was a source of tension between them. He adored the British, vehemently disagreeing with Jamaica being independent.

Although, he understood that it was mainly economic difficulties that led many people to migrate including himself, he regularly said, " I don't see what there is to love about Jamaica anyway."

However Daisy was determined to return to her home country to live the kind of life she had always wanted, with the pension she earned from her job as a cook in a local hospital kitchen.

She was able to build a house with hers and my father's wages combined and to become someone of significance back home, not, as she was, the woman struggling in poverty to raise her siblings.

Daisy died ten years after moving back to Jamaica. I went to her funeral, which was, some years ago. Despite the way she had mistreated me, I felt compelled to. I was in Jamaica on holiday and was told she had died. As I sat at the back of the church, I saw further evidence of how one person could be both extremely good and cruel at the same time. I saw how deeply she loved and was loved. I saw the striking figures of her over-six-foot tall brothers all with white hair and beards and her sons and a grandson carrying her coffin into the church. They were overwhelmed with grief, mourning the loss of their beloved sister, mother and grandmother.

I noticed that one after another, people talked about her tremendous generosity, her positive contribution to their lives. It was incredible. According to the people who spoke at the funeral, she was a saint, yet she had shown no compassion for another woman's child, for me.

I sat there contemplating,

*Was it just poverty and desperation that led her to mistreat me or was it jealousy? Perhaps it was both.*

# My Goals

In 1984, I left my job in the global American company Monsanto when they moved to another part of the country. I still have the reference the manager wrote.

'Pam has decided to embark upon a new career in sociology. Those who have had the pleasure of knowing her will readily appreciate that this is no passing fancy but is founded on a genuine desire to render assistance to those in need, from which she will derive a greater feeling of job satisfaction.'

How well he knew me, better than my own father did. I received redundancy pay, which I used for my living expenses while I pursued my mission to become a social worker.

By now, after much pleading from me, Fitz and I were living together. He was no great financial contributor, but that didn't matter to me, our bond was what was important. The fact that I had to beg him to move in with me bothered me but, as I believed there was something wrong with me and I was unworthy, I accepted it. I didn't think there could be any other reason that he was reluctant to live with me, even after he bought me an engagement ring but never spoke about getting married.

Ready now to pursue my career, I made enquiries about how I could become a social worker in my local borough. They had a preparatory course for people wanting to train for that career. Driven by absolute determination, I had no doubt that I'd get on the course and after the interview, I was offered a place.

On that course, I met some of my best friends whom I have kept to this day. We are all united in our pain and triumph over the adversity of our childhood experiences.

Interestingly, my main tutor was also from my parish of St. Thomas in Jamaica. He set about helping us to understand our history and the cultural context in which we would be working in the UK. The teachers introduced us to essay writing and challenged us in many ways to build our confidence and to understand what was expected of us at university.

I was successful in getting a place at North East London University, and I met other friends there of all cultures. Some who had similar types of experiences to me and others whose experiences although different had an impact on them. But we all had something that drove us to want to become social workers.

We knew we could make a difference and become champions for children and vulnerable people, steeped in the understanding that our experiences had afforded us. We possessed the added knowledge of social policy and many theories, including Bowlby's attachment theory, philosophy, group-work, behavioural psychology, change and systemic theories, community work concepts, and psychoanalysis.

My main tutor had a psychoanalytical leaning, which meant he understood the usefulness of our past experiences and that we needed to acknowledge and use them to understand how to help our clients. The result of this, for me, was the beginning of self-awareness and explicitly understanding emotional intelligence.

My fellow students and I couldn't wait to set about making our impact, causing positive change for the people we worked with. I studied day and night, using an old typewriter, and my friend 'Tippex'. I am certain my fingers grew muscles using that typewriter. No 'golf ball' typewriter for me, I couldn't afford such a modern piece of equipment. There was no computer, we didn't even have those at work yet. I stayed up all night crying over my homework, wanting to make sure that I finished it and got a good mark.

By the time I passed the social work course, I had bought a yellow car with the gear stick in the dashboard. I think back on that old Renault with fondness. I used to give my friends at university lifts in it. They still talk about the number of times we got lost!

On this course, I met another young man, Kenneth. In many ways, he reminded me of my Uncle John. He was the same height, and complexion, and treated me as a precious gem. This was strange, not an experience I had ever had before in my adult life. I frequently felt his piercing eyes whenever we were in close proximity.

"He's obsessed with you," my classmates whispered.

"Haven't you noticed how he looks at you and hangs on to your every word? Have you seen how he watches you walk?"

I knew he liked me and I was secretly enjoying the experience. We used the opportunity of the lifts home I gave him, to talk and, one day, I agreed to visit him for a meal. Over dinner, he told me about his feelings for me.

I had never felt this level of adoration, and it made me feel uncomfortable. I didn't tell him that I felt awkward because I wondered if this attention was really what was good for me. Throughout the years of our course, his interest never waned.

On another day after we had a meal and we were walking to the bus stop, he paused for a minute and in his gentle voice he asked, "Pam, would you consider marrying me?"

He was so sincere that I felt emotionally overwhelmed for a minute or two before I replied, "I don't know, let me think about it."

In the days before I saw him again, I gave his proposal serious thought. I had a clear positive picture about what life would be like with him from our conversations and I knew he loved me.

But again, when it came to it, I couldn't leave Fitz. I was sure that if Kenneth knew everything about me, he couldn't possibly want me. This was my thinking, even though I shared some of my life-story with him and he didn't recoil. He had even revealed some of his past to me, which made me realise we had some experiences in common.

A major factor in me deciding not to choose him was that I was not convinced he could protect me, protection being a vital requirement of any man in my life. My evidence for this was an incident that happened before he asked me to marry him.

One summer's evening I dropped Kenneth home from university and was parked outside his house as we talked. A little while after, I looked in my rear-view mirror and saw that Fitz was parked behind my car. I watched as he rushed out of his car and headed towards us. With my heart pounding, I shrieked, "Fitz is behind us. He is running towards us."

I looked at Kenneth and saw that he was scared. Not knowing what else to do, I drove off with him still sitting in the passenger seat. When we reached the end of the road, Kenneth asked me to let him out. I stopped the car and he got out. I watched him, with his head bowed walk past Fitz who was shouting expletives through his car window at Kenneth and he didn't say anything back. What did I expect? I wanted him to speak up for me, and he didn't.

I drove home with Fitz following behind me in his car. Fitz started an argument about what he saw. I maintained that I was talking to my friend reminding Fitz that he had no right to talk to me about this, given that he promised to and had not married me.

I never felt the same about Kenneth after this, because an important measure of love for me was that you could defend me, and he didn't show me that he could. So, I decided to stay with Fitz and make it work.

When I was twenty-nine, we decided to have a child. After our son was born, I contacted my father to tell him he had a grandchild. I was so happy to have my son that I wanted everyone to know. Although I was fully aware of Vernon's limitations, I thought that it was better for my son to know his grandfather than not to know him at all.

A week before my son was one year old, I left him with Fitz and I drove to where my father lived in

Brixton. As I arrived at the door, I recalled that fateful night 13 years previous, when they blocked me from entering the flat. I hesitated for a moment then knocked determinedly, still filled with the joy of having my son, feeling responsible for his experience of life. I had a burning desire for him not to grow up without family, the way that I did. I knew there was a risk they'd close the door in my face, but I owed it to my son to try.

Daisy answered the door, "Oh, hello!" she gasped.

"Hi, is my father here?" I asked.

She turned and called out "Vernon! Your daughter is here!"

My father came to the door, with a half-smile and a look of surprise.

"Come in," he said.

I went in and we sat down in the kitchen. I pretended nothing had gone on before and proceeded to tell him that he had a grandson.

He looked genuinely happy and asked, "When was he born? What's his name? Where is he?"

Vernon called to Daisy, who had gone upstairs.

"Come here, you hear the news? I have a grandson."

She came down and stood at the entrance to the living room.

"Is that so?" she turned to me and smiled. "Who him look like?"

I didn't reply but gave them an invitation to my son's first birthday party and left.

When Vernon turned up at the birthday party, he was clearly happy to meet, his grandson. Fitz and he were cordial to each other that day. Friends who were there met my father for the first time.

Both Vernon and Daisy appeared to somehow block out the memory of what they did to me and what they had said about me in Jamaica when they tried to paint me as being immoral. Perhaps they thought I didn't know.

My step-mother even baked the birthday cake my father brought to my son's first birthday party. We were all pretending, at least to some extent.

But with Vernon and Daisy more so than anyone else, I was like a mother hen protector. My personal experience gave me a consciousness about what adults can do to children. I never let my son out of my sight when we visited my father, although he was always charming. My son benefited because he got to know the good side of his grandfather and, for that, I am happy.

Soon after my son was born, Aunt Dar, died at home in Jamaica. I was told that she went to lie down during the day and died in her sleep. I believe her blood pressure was high, the result of stress caused by her third husband, another philanderer. He had been staying away from home with a girlfriend, an embarrassing fact known by everyone. Despite the benefits Aunt Dar's status and background gave him, he sought a place where he could be the dominant figure. The poverty his much younger girlfriend was experiencing meant that she needed him and made him feel important and valued, something he struggled to achieve with my great-aunt.

I was at work when someone, I don't remember who, came to tell me that she had passed away. I was very distraught. Despite the obvious fact that I knew she was not going to live forever, I was not prepared for this eventuality. Frozen, I cried before my autopilot kicked in and I started thinking about what I needed to do next.

I walked into my bank across the road from the office and explained to the bank manager that I simply had to go to the funeral. I needed the fare and more. He was wonderful and loaned me the money. I repaid it from my salary every month after that. Isn't it interesting what buys lifetime loyalty? They remain my bank to this day because of this.

Sadly, Aunt Dar never met my beautiful baby. I took him with me to Jamaica and set about securing her burial. It was interesting that all the people my great-aunt looked after didn't feel they had to help with financing her funeral. I guess they thought she was rich and that she gave it all to me. They were so wrong. She didn't die leaving a lot of money at all.

Learning about my culture's burial rituals was an experience; the expectations for 'nine nights' of gatherings before the funeral. There wasn't that much help as I tried to understand and arrange it all. I later found out I could have bought a burial package from the funeral parlour. That's not to say I'd have done this, as I don't think I'd have been forgiven for the insult local people would have felt had I taken away their opportunity to be part of the ritual. It was a chance to reminisce and partake in the free food and drink provided over the nine nights to anyone coming to the house where the dead person had lived. For people in poverty, this is a big deal.

I inherited Aunt Dar's home, the house where the beatings took place. To this day I cannot find comfort in this inheritance, because it felt like her way of compensating me for the beating. My great-aunt did a strange thing too, she left the forty-plus acres of land in Orange Park that her father gave her, to one of her godson's, a lawyer whom she had arranged to marry me as a condition of his inheritance.

That was never going to happen. I knew him as a child and, some years before her death, I met up with him in London when she first wrote her will. He was returning to Jamaica after having qualified as a lawyer. We talked about me returning to live in St Thomas but not explicitly about me being with him. In any case, I had Fitz, who knew and accepted me.

After Aunt Dar died, my father and his wife eventually returned to live in Jamaica. Despite being unhappy that Aunt Dar left me her house, my father did his best to keep an eye out for it. He even went to court after my great-aunt's husband, who I left living there, falsely accused him of burning valuables he didn't have. He made these accusations after my father emptied and burned the contents of her bedroom when termites had taken over.

During this time, my father and I were in communication and I even visited Jamaica while he was there. All of us, Vernon, Daisy and I, didn't talk about my time living with them, his sexual abuse or their behaviour afterwards. I think that they knew that Aunt Dar had told me what they said about me. But not one of us acknowledged or revealed this.

One day during this period, after a therapy session, I decided to write him a letter. I told him everything I held in about them. There were no kind words in that letter. Communication stopped for a while until the day when he needed me to help him handle a legal matter. After that, we never spoke about the letter. However, for my healing, it was vital that I sent it to him. Writing that letter helped me to believe that what he did to me was not just in my mind. Seeing the words on paper that I had only ever spoken before, was powerful. It released some of the pressure I felt inside and helped me to feel freer from the past than ever before.

# Awakenings

Before I had my son, I qualified as a social worker and was working in the role. At this time, I decided to push Fitz into achieving his potential. We agreed that he didn't have to work to contribute financially to the household while he attended his classes because he needed the time to study. For a year, at around the age of forty, Fitz worked a bit and said he went to college the rest of the time.

On one of the days when he was taking his exam, I decided I'd come home early and cook a meal with wine to celebrate his achievement. I understood it wasn't easy for him to put aside all his feelings about being an older student.

I went to the supermarket and bought fish, his favourite thing to eat. I hurried home to get back before he did, calculating that his exam would end at 4:30 pm. and it would take an hour for him to drive home so I had time to surprise him, especially as I wasn't usually the cook, he was. I approached and didn't see his car parked outside, so I knew I'd made it home before him. Struggling with my bags up the stairs to the flat, I opened the door.

Sitting in the chair at the dining table was Fitz, smoking a cigarette, something I thought he never did in the house.

Surprised, I asked, "What are you doing home so early?"

He looked at me and said, "Studying is for young people."

I was disappointed and upset, a whole year of a lie because he couldn't tell me, he was too embarrassed. To be fair, I was pushing him that hard it would not have been easy for him to tell me. I wasn't listening to the non-verbal cues. I don't know if he ever went to college at all.

We continued our relationship nonetheless, but some of the sheen had gone. I doubled down and thought,

*Well Pam, that's not going to happen. He isn't going to achieve his aspirations, but you are in this, you love him, so just keep going. This is the man you are going to marry one day and live the rest of your life with.*

We kept going for years, talking about him doing better but this was not happening.

Instead, I did better, buying my house and moving up through the career ladder. The one thing that dulled my existence was the fact that, despite his promise that we could be married, we never did it. I buried how this fact left me feeling and 'toughed it out' again until after my son was born.

Having my son helped me to see clearly the situation that I was in. It was strange, becoming a mother affected my perspective, in a way I never ever expected. I wanted the best for my child and saw that the example of mum and dad together, in the way that Fitz and I were, was not the best.

By now, Fitz was struggling with my career progression, not obstructing, but not endorsing it either. It didn't matter much to me. I was on my unstoppable mission to make a difference. His feelings, linked to his sense of inadequacy, were just a nagging hum in the background.

Another factor that helped me was that I saw clearly that I independently could look after my son and myself financially. I always could because of my efforts but somehow before, it felt like I couldn't without Fitz. It wasn't true, it was my perception that Fitz had helped to build, by some of the things he said. He had manipulative tendencies like my father, albeit subtler. For my part, of course, I could be manipulated given my vulnerability and needs.

Over time, I also discovered I didn't need the 'protection' that I thought Fitz represented. The cloud had lifted, and I chose not to 'tough it out' anymore. So, we drifted apart.

Over many months, we stopped being civil to each other, even though we were still living together. Losing respect for him, I'd point out his short-comings and he would become angry. One day, this culminated in him spitting at me during an argument.

For me, that was the final straw. I told him to get out of my house. He knew I meant it and left but not before saying,

"You won't manage without me, just watch. Who will turn off the gas fire in the mornings now?"

I thought, *Wow, was that the sum of your contribution to us?*

We both knew it was far more than that, but in the heat of the moment, that is all he could think to say.

When we broke up, Fitz returned to his wife. Yes, she was his wife, he eventually admitted it after she, somewhat belatedly, wrote to tell me this. In response to her letter, he said he always felt I'd outgrow him. This was his excuse for lying all those years.

However, to be honest, I didn't investigate the story about him being married because I had other needs. Also, the same way I was afraid to know whether my mother wanted me, I was afraid to know explicitly that Fitz didn't want me for the long-term and didn't think me good enough to marry.

He recently told me he had the best years of his life with me and I am certain he did. For the buffer and support he provided, I am grateful. For the lies he told, I forgive him. It's behind me now.

# My Father's Demise

Now living as a single mother, I concentrated on making my way up the professional ladder and giving my son what he needed to be whole. One day while at work, I received a phone call from someone who was the daughter of one of my father's friends.

"Your father is at my father's house, and he's sick!" she cried.

"He's asking for you. I looked you up and found you!"

"What!?" I asked, exasperated. "What's he doing here? When did he arrive? Is he on his own?"

She told me the address and after work, I went to see him. He looked emaciated and fragile. I nearly didn't recognise the man who greeted me.

"Hello Pam," he muttered.

It wasn't hard to be sorry for him because his eyes were pleading for help, his head was bowed low and his thin body shaking.

Vernon said he was okay, but he clearly wasn't. He had become acutely ill. I set about helping him to get treatment, but it was a torrid time.

The house was poorly heated in the middle of winter. There was no one to cook for him, so I had to make sure he ate and kept warm. Eventually, I took him to the hospital. After admission, I discovered that he was dehydrated, which contributed to his confused state.

Some years earlier in Jamaica, he left my step-mother when she started to develop dementia. He built himself a house by the seaside and had a young helper, who also became his girlfriend.

A situation like this is not uncommon in the Caribbean and many other countries where deprivation is prevalent. For this young woman, desperate to feed and educate her children out of the poverty trap, a man like my father was a gift. His pensions could help send the two children she had before she met him, to school. In return, she looked after him and his house and fulfilled his need for a woman in his life.

When I telephoned his step-son, my step-mother's other son, Frank, to ask what happened to my father, he claimed nothing had, he was alright.

He said he had been looking out for him after he left his mother. Vernon's condition when he arrived in the UK did not confirm that he had been well looked after at all, not by Frank or by the helper-cum-girlfriend.

Vernon told me he thought he had prostate cancer, a diagnosis that was never confirmed. In any case, after a while, he recovered and desperately wanted to return to Jamaica.

While he was ill my father asked me for Fitz, this was strange to hear and by then Fitz and I were broken up. But as we were still cordial, seeing each other when he visited our son, I told Fitz, and he visited him. They seemed to get on fine, which in a strange way helped me to share the burden of responsibility for my father. Each of them knew about the other's role in my life.

While Vernon was recovering, I placed him in a private residential home because I did not want him living with me. Then, true to form, just when I said I'd take time off work to take him back to Jamaica but not on the dates he wanted, he told the staff at the home that I was refusing to take him back home to see his girlfriend. He lied, continuing his practice of smearing my reputation.

Not able to bear his manipulation, I hurriedly sent him back, accompanied by a friend of his, who happened to be going to Jamaica at that time. He was no longer very confused but still an old man that wasn't steady on his feet. I was glad to be rid of him and I telephoned his girlfriend in Jamaica to ask her to take good care of him. Before he went, he told me that he wanted me to give up work to look after him.

"After all," he insisted, "that's why I stopped your mother aborting you. You were supposed to look after me in my old age."

*What is he talking about?* I thought. *Is this man crazy? Me? Give up my career to look after you?*

It never occurred to him that I had any hopes of my own. It was only what he wanted that mattered. I know this is not uncommon, but it still hurt after all I had gone through.

I didn't even tell him that I was an Assistant Director of social services at the time, striving to make my contribution to children in the greatest way possible.

Vernon died eight years after first returning to Jamaica with Daisy. I got the chance to see him just before he passed away. I heard that he told anyone walking past his house that his daughter had abandoned him, and he regularly stood at his gate looking for me. He fixated on his desire for me to come and care for him.

Vernon died a torturous death, a death no one should ever have. My step-brother told me that he was just a little ill. Suspecting this was not entirely true, I asked someone living in Jamaica to go visit him to tell me about his condition. The person told me he was in the hospital, not at home!

Why did I ask someone else to check on Vernon? I had become suspicious of my step-brother because of the state my father was in when he turned up in the UK.

I didn't think he genuinely cared about my father. To me, it seemed he was keeping a watchful eye on him for other reasons. I didn't have the time or the imagination to work out exactly what the reason was, I was just suspicious.

The woman who visited Vernon told me he was in fact gravely ill and most probably dying. I didn't know what he was dying of, but if he was dying, I had to see him. This was my only living parent and, despite his behaviour, he was my father and my son's grandfather. It wasn't the ideal time to leave work because of some issues that were occurring in the organisation, but I had to go. I was not going to miss the funeral like I did when my mother and my sister died. I told work I was going and off I went. I got the plane to Jamaica and went straight to the public hospital.

I found Vernon lying on the bed with his hands tied to the bedposts with dirty pieces of torn clothes.

This man, who was such a meticulous dresser, was lying in dirty pyjamas with both the top and bottom wide open, revealing his genital area where I and everyone else could see that the first layer of skin there had peeled off.

It had become so irritated when his urine burnt him that he kept trying to dig at it. The nurses said that was why they had tied his hands, to stop him. He was trying to get his hands free but couldn't, he was too weak. He was delirious and in an horrendous state. There were moments when he calmed down a little and stopped rocking his head from side to side and out of breath,

"Where... have... you... been?

I need... to... tell... you... something." He stuttered

"What is it?" I asked.

"The... will... we... have... to... go... see... a lawyer," he muttered.

"Don't worry about that now," I reassured him.

Sometimes I didn't understand what he was saying, it was merely the incoherent rantings of a man in distress.

It seemed to me that everyone had abandoned him. The nurses were busy with other patients, perhaps those who needed them more. They had nothing like the resources needed.

I didn't care, this was not acceptable to me. I looked at him and thought,

*Oh God, no! He needs help, my only living parent needs help!*

He needed something for whatever was causing him to dig at his genitals. He also required clean bedding, underwear and pyjamas that could be tied at the waist.

His hands had to be untied. Nobody around seemed to meet my expected standards which I, thought were basic. It turned out, in that context, my standards were in fact high.

The step-brother and my father's girlfriend seemed to be passively looking on, bringing him juice, but not ensuring that he could drink it nor checking whether juice was the right thing for him to drink.

I don't know what happened to them, I think his girlfriend was in shock, paralysed by the potential loss and the impact on her livelihood. For my step-brother, I couldn't shake off my original belief that he just didn't care.

I bounced into being the manager of everyone in sight.

"Go home and bring him some clean clothes and bedding," I directed his girlfriend.

"Can't you help him?" I pleaded with the nurses. "Give him some pain relief, please give him something! He's in agony?"

My irritation was not just with them, but with the fact that I had to be there with him and that I had no choice but to help him again.

It wasn't easy to get a conversation that resulted in what I wanted from the nurses. And, certainly not by the way I was asking for help. I eventually found someone senior in the hospital who knew our family name and background, the key to getting good service in an overstretched environment!

Over the next two weeks, I calmed down, resigned to my task, to my responsibility. I drove to the hospital in my rental car every day, watching my father toss, turn and twist.

Vernon never spoke again, only communicating with his eyes, that blue circle surrounding his pupils almost completely replacing the brown now. He lay silently looking at me as a vulnerable, helpless child would or a puppy that needed help. He had no more words to paint me in a bad light or confuse me, no ability to take actions to hurt me.

As I watched him, I thought about all the things he had said and done to me. I thought about how much he frustrated me and how powerless I felt to stop him. My memory of the sexual abuse was still clouded by my misguided belief that I might have caused it.

But, I also remembered the good things like the laughter, how he lit up a room and how much he gave me by telling me about my mother. It's not the case that everything about abusers is bad. It's easy for us to think this but it's not true. It is the mixed picture of them that makes it difficult for the abused. We do a disservice to the abused not to acknowledge this.

One day I was sitting with Vernon, thinking about work, when I noticed his bedding needed changing.

*I'll just do it,* I thought. My, oh my, what an error! I planned to do one part of the bed first, then the other. He almost fell off the bed!

"Nurse, Nurse help me!" I cried.

I couldn't lift him back up. He was as heavy as lead, the weight of a man nearly deceased. Thank God a nurse came! I felt so terrible at the time, but I laugh about it now. It was a ridiculous situation to get myself into. Imagine thinking you could move a man that is almost dead.

Another day, I was sitting with Vernon, and his mouth started moving rapidly, but there was no sound. I watched him and saw his despair, just air instead of the words as he tried to speak. No sound, no false teeth, just a thin, emaciated man, his head rocking from side to side. So much distress. It was too much for me. In that moment, I felt a painful compassion for him. I watched him and felt his agony, his fear. Without thinking, I found myself whispering to him,

"It's Okay, I forgive you. You can go."

I don't know what effect this had, but he quieted down after that and I sat with him a while longer before I left. Early the next morning, I received a phone call saying he was dead.

I wailed and wailed, I had never cried like that before. I wept for the loss of a parent and for the turmoil he put me through, for the fact that I was now an orphan. I wept for all my losses.

Soon after I went to see him in the morgue. A slab on a tray, this is what he was reduced to. A body without its spirit is only flesh and bones. This hit me deeply. This is what humans are? Not a powerful anything, they only behave as though they are, and they count on others believing it. Obvious really, but until I saw the separation of energy, the life gone from my father's body, I didn't appreciate this.

My father was saved by the fact that I am someone with compassion for human beings, perhaps linked to the compassion I was forced to have for myself when I was being tortured by my great-aunt and raped and sexually abused. I am glad I told him I forgave him before he went. I am lighter for it. It was part of putting it behind me. This is what forgiveness is.

After Vernon died, I saw how much my brother Oliver hated him.

I set about burying him because no one else would. My father's wife, Daisy, from whom he had separated, was ill with dementia. His step-son Frank had no real interest. My sister-mother, his daughter, had died long before and my other siblings were not his children.

*What else could I do? Who else will do it?*

I asked Oliver to come to Jamaica, if not for our father's sake, for mine. He agreed, only if I paid his airfare. I paid it, and he arrived in Jamaica from Spain where he was living with his family. I literally leaned on him for the support I needed during the funeral.

I selected a flashy-looking coffin for Vernon befitting of his style. I felt I had to do that, still influenced by appearances, still concerned about what the people who loved him thought and said.

As I sat in the church, it occurred to me again that the person, the big personality, the spirit was gone. Oliver helped me during that ceremony. He accompanied me to the pulpit where I read the eulogy that I had written, full of the things people recognised and liked about my father.

I reminded them of his favourite phrases. "Boy, oh Boy!" was one of the sayings he used at the beginning of any sentence, if he was excited when declaring anything. I included other expressions that Vernon used and delivered them in his style and tone. The congregation smiled, and some cried. I talked about how much fun he was, never mentioning that he was a confused man.

I cried as I read the eulogy partly because it was so hard to do. Oliver's support helped me to endure the burial afterwards. At the graveside, I found myself crying for the death of a mother I never knew, crying about not being able to let go of my father until now. My tears flowed about his manipulation of me but also about the finality that his positive energy was no longer around.

I stood there carrying the secret shame of what he did to me and having to keep up appearances by not saying anything about it. I also knew that people believed I should have looked after him in his old age and I didn't. I left the graveside and went home, feeling weary. I closed my gate and door to the people who wanted to continue the burial ritual. I decided I could not cope with what I imagined were their views about me, not this time.

That very same day Oliver and his half-brother (my step-brother Frank), came to see me. Frank's words revealed that he was riddled with jealousy because his mother left and took Oliver to England with her, leaving him behind, albeit in his father's more affluent household. He was making Oliver pay for it now by dominating him. Oliver, the same person who had just finished supporting me, was beset with hatred for my father and had found a perfect bedfellow. They both told me what they thought should happen to my father's property.

"Well, Pam, I have decided what needs to happen now that your father is dead," Frank instructed me, condescendingly.

"Oliver and I will rightfully inherit this house. We are entitled to it. You have enough anyway. You have your rich family in America, your life in England and you have a property here already."

Indignant with the nerve they had to gang up on me, to try to intimidate me at this time, I rounded on them.

I don't know where I found the strength to deliver the stinging words, telling them exactly what they were really angry about. I told them about their transference of their own and their mother's anger. I told them everything I had ever wanted to tell them. I had no fear.

It's interesting that all this was released by my father's death. Finally feeling absolutely fearless, I went up close to those two men and told them to get the hell away from me. And, they did!

I felt like I was finally fighting back against every unfairness I had ever experienced, every injustice. I was prepared for anything.

*Enough!* I thought. *No more! I will die fighting for my right not to be abused or taken advantage of anymore.*

I meant it too. I knew it was this stance that sent them on their way.

After that, I arranged for security bars to be placed all around my father's house, especially in my father's apartment on the side of the building.

I left the tenant on the other side of the house with instructions not to let my step-brother anywhere near the house. I found an unsigned will and kept it. For seven years after my father died, I paid the land tax and occasionally went there on holiday. My idea for the future of the house was that my son and the nieces and nephews including my brother's children would one day have it as a holiday home.

It's strange what grief brings out in people. My brother's betrayal and all the other factors made me finally fight back. The extent to which I was in touch with my emotions during this time was unprecedented. We were all angry and experiencing raw emotions, perhaps never to be felt so acutely again.

Oliver was still so resentful of my mother's place in our father's heart, of the impact on his mother, and our father's earlier neglect of him as a child. We were three angry people for different, yet inter-connected reasons.

We fought verbally for years before I finally decided I did not need to continue to carry on my parent's battles. I didn't need to be fighting about a house that symbolised other people's wars. I needed to be free of the past. Thus, I didn't respond when I heard that my step-brother had gained access and proceeded to move one of his children and the mother there.

I recently heard that they sold the property. They continue to revel in what they think was a victory for their mother. Yet, I revel in the freedom them taking the house has given me, the lightness I now feel not continuing with the conflict that began with our parents. You need at least two opposing sides for a war, and I finally removed myself from the fight.

# Parenting

It was interesting having my son. I wanted to have a baby because I figured I knew what children needed. You see, I was always a child who knew, at some level, that what my parent figures did was wrong. I had that internal antenna. I decided that, when I had my own child, I would not repeat what any of them did.

I knew that, as a child, I needed to be told I was loved, so number one on my agenda was to tell him I loved him. I wasn't just telling him this either. I was going to ensure that he felt loved.

To my mind, it was clear that any child I had, above all else, needed to know they were important. They needed to feel they were special (that's what I got from the way Uncle John treated me). I remembered the good feeling I had when I felt special. I knew it helped with my resilience.

I worked hard to give my son the best 'mothering' I could. I had him after I trained to be a social worker and I used everything I'd learnt. I had a child development book about what behaviours to expect from children at different ages, and this became my bible. When my son behaved in a way I didn't understand, it helped to read about what I should expect from a child at specific stages such as needing to detach from me in adolescence. I could see the reasons for his actions and regulated my responses accordingly. This, coupled with how in touch I was with the child in me, helped.

His words and actions told me when I was being overbearing and needed to trust that I had taught him enough and that he could make decisions himself. I had to curb my inclination to tell him who to be friendly with and celebrated when he worked it out for himself.

One day, when he was about fifteen, some of his friends were visiting. I had to go out, but when I came back, I saw him sitting on the stairs looking angrier than I had ever seen him.

"What's wrong?" I asked.

He glared for a moment then replied. "Mom, can you believe Adam thought it was okay to put his feet on our glass table and to open the door to your room? I kicked them out!"

I am still proud to this day.

From my own experience, I knew that being over-controlled could lead to increased curiosity and vulnerability, so I applied what I can only call 'intelligent parenting.' I knew what my son could do in advance of him doing it, and I'd head it off by occupying him or engaging with him. My deflecting techniques were honed. On most occasions, I got it right and, the times where I was wrong, my son and I now laugh about them together. One time, when he was eighteen, he came into my bedroom and sat at the end of the bed, waking me up.

"Mom, I have something to tell you," he muttered, pained.

I looked at him and wondered what it could be. I said the only thing I could think of at the time.

"Darling, if you are going to tell me you are gay, it's fine. I love you whatever your sexuality."

He glared at me incredulously. "Mom, why say that? What indication did I ever give you of that?"

"Nothing darling," I soothed. "I just thought that was why you were so upset."

"I wasn't upset," he insisted, "I was going to tell you something important!"

For the rest of the day he walked around the house being 'camp'. I was very embarrassed when he eventually told me that he came to tell me about an important event in his maturity.

I worked at building the type of relationship where my son could tell me anything. Through his upbringing, we communicated in a way that I did not experience when I was a child.

Like some parents, I have set about filling the gaps in the way I was parented, addressing the issues and safeguarding him from the abuses I had suffered. I'd regularly examine myself to ensure that I did not replicate the poor parenting style of my own caregivers, whilst also capitalising and building on their positive attributes.

This wasn't easy because I had to strike a balance. I was mindfully aware that the pendulum should not swing from one extreme to the other, I needed not to overcompensate.

I gave my son rules and ensured he knew the significance of them. I knew he needed to be occupied. Not just with his academic schoolwork, which his father and I helped with. For his holistic development he also needed sports activities and the arts, he tried them all.

I knew that he needed to have a relationship with his father but that he needed to know the entire truth. I also understood that he needed others to contribute to his knowledge and understanding of the world. It is evident that this has helped me.

His godmothers made a perfect contribution. They were my friends in whom I had confided over the years. Together we shared our experiences about the parenting we received and did not want to impart. They did the things I wasn't good at. They talked and exposed him to things I was hesitant to address.

Once, one of his godmothers gave him a shoebox for his birthday. I thought it was a pair of trainers or something similar. When I thanked her for it, she said, "Yes, it's what every young man should have." Unsure why she was saying this about shoes I ignored it.

Sometime later, when she was talking to me, she added, "I hope he uses the condoms."

I was beside myself. He was only twelve. I didn't want him exposed to this already. It turned out that this was the perfect time to plant the importance of safe sex in his young mind. My son and I still laugh about his godmother's boldness, and how she got through my barriers by disguising her actions.

Another godmother showed her love for him through all the creative writing tools and books she gave him over the years. She decided how she wanted to contribute to him and she consistently achieved it. My son and I are both very grateful to them. I knew that not only a Mom and Dad were needed, it really does take a whole village to raise a healthy child.

Even Aunt Dar contributed to my son. Throughout his life prompted by what she said to me at a young age, I told and showed him that he could be anything he wanted to be.

Every child needs good role models and mentors. My son's black male martial arts teachers made an invaluable contribution to him and are his role models to this day. I knew that it was possible to bring up a child without beatings. I understood that we needed to acknowledge feelings and to talk things through.

I wasn't perfect, but I felt that I didn't have all those experiences for me not to know how to bring up a child. I took parenting very seriously. I am thankful that he was and still is confident enough to tell me when I fall short. I got over most of my disinclination to take advice from my child.

It wasn't easy and I often thought,

*I am the parent, the adult. How could a child contribute to me?*

He told me that this was disrespectful of him.

Locking him down in a role that was always subordinate to me was robbing me of the value of his 'line of sight', the value of youth, the freshness and energy young people bring.

In allowing him to help me, I benefit from the immense value of the clarity of his mind, his considerable skills and insight. My disinclination to listen to him still pops up from time to time, but I know I rob myself of his contribution to me when I do this. Thankfully, he is too strong to allow me to do this, he insists on contributing. He 'calls me out' when I am regressing into the parent-child relationship.

My son, who at the time of writing is twenty-nine years of age, is a formidable human being. He resolves issues quickly. I first understood who he was when he obtained information about his siblings from his father. Information that I had failed to get for him over many years. He then, contacted them himself, satisfying his curiosity and theirs.

This outstanding contributor to humanity is whom I now have as a son. Why do I describe him in this way? This is a young man who guides anyone he encounters, building his or her self-belief, whether these people are friends or people he mentors or manages. He is a natural teacher, is very motivating and contributes to others in a way I could never have imagined.

I am confident that he is going to be an awesome father and a better parent than I. I hope I am still here to support his children who will learn from him, building on what he learnt from me.

I celebrate the fact that I did not repeat the abusive parenting I received. I know you do not have to copy what you experience, and I also know that to break the pattern, you have to work hard on yourself, relentlessly. Only by doing so, can we break the chains that bind us to the past.

# A Wife

When my son went to university, I had time to think about my life. Finally, it dawned on me that I wanted to have a partner. I thought about my childhood neighbour, Trevor.

Over the years, we had ongoing contact when I visited Jamaica. We had talked about marrying each other if we weren't married by the time our children were grown up. We both held each other in reserve!

Trevor had previously visited me in England, staying with his brothers and sisters who, it turned out, lived near me.

When he next visited, we decided we liked each other enough to honour our promise to marry. For me, he was a connection to my past. Most of all, he was someone who accepted me enough to make a long-term commitment. As far as I was concerned at the time, all boxes were ticked. He was my man.

The wedding happened quickly after our decision. I didn't discuss it with my son, who by now was living with his girlfriend. It was strange not talking to my son about this, given the closeness of our relationship, but I was too fired up about doing something just for me. I anticipated and felt my son's scepticism but I was on a mission. I also felt the disapproval of my friends'. They all loved me and didn't want me to make a mistake. But I ignored them and galloped into the marriage.

Trevor and I got married on a cold day in November 2011. I wore a hurriedly bought dress and a fur stole that I inherited from my sister Loretta. The stole represented my family at the wedding because I hadn't told them about it or invited them. On the big day, I arrived at the church, accompanied by my son who was giving me away, and my beautiful goddaughter, the flower girl.

As I walked down the aisle, I saw Trevor standing at the altar with his best man. Sitting in the church were his family and my friends. As I stood beside him, nervous and overwhelmed by the fact that I was accepted, I couldn't repeat the words the vicar spoke. Trevor, holding my hand, prompted me and, eventually, I repeated them.

"I, Pam Rowe, take you Trevor McKenzie to be my husband, to have and to hold from this day forward, for better or worse, for richer or poorer..."

After that, I was continuously smiling and crying with happiness like I had never done before.

The reception that I arranged was perfect. As we sat at the head table surrounded by our guests in the beautiful glass encased room adorned with flowers, I listened to Trevor's speech.

"I would like to, first of all, thank the chef for cooking the best curry goat I have eaten outside of Jamaica." To raucous applause, he raised his glass and said, "To my family and friends, I know you are happy that I have finally settled down." In closing, he lamented, "I am really sorry my children can't be here today." He sat back down beside me smiling with joy.

Trevor didn't refer to me, which I was hoping for and was a little embarrassed about the omission. I had imagined him professing his undying love for me in front of our guests. Why did I expect this when he never did this before? Because it was my fairy tale fantasy, that this wedding and marriage was going to be all I ever wanted.

We hadn't arranged a honeymoon immediately after the wedding because we planned to go to Jamaica a few months later. But, a couple of nights after we married, he told me a friend of his was having a party and we should go. A little nervous about our first outing as husband and wife, I got dressed and off we went. At the party there were many people from our district back home in St Thomas, Jamaica, who were very friendly with Trevor. I didn't know them and was introduced to them as his wife.

To my mind, the women were over-friendly with him and slightly mean to me. At first, I thought I was imagining it, but this was confirmed throughout the two hours that I sat watching. He was enjoying himself while I sat talking to another guest who seemed to be an outsider like myself, uncomfortable in this unfamiliar environment.

As the night went on, they offered him food, and he went to get it, passing me by, not asking if I wanted any. Later as I sat watching, he started dancing with one of the hosts in what was too intimate a manner. Unable to tolerate this, I picked up my bag and coat and went to wait in the car. He came out around half an hour later.

"Pam, what's wrong?"

"You have brought me to one of your ex-girlfriend's houses and allowed her to disrespect me and you've disrespected me too." I retorted.

He listened and then merely said, "I'm sorry."

He didn't explain things any further, and we never talked about it again. What it did for me though was cause me to begin to understand who he was.

When we went to Jamaica on our honeymoon, we had a good time, but I had another opportunity to notice his selfishness. I decided that, as I was bearing all the expenses, the least he could do was finance our meals, especially given the fact that some of his family there were farmers.

We didn't really discuss this, I simply told him to pay for the food we ate. He struggled to do this, and, on one occasion, he brought home a meal given to him by his family.

"This is my breakfast," he said and placed it in the fridge. I asked him if some of it was for me and he said no, it was for him alone.

There was another time that I was in the supermarket and just before I paid for the groceries, he whispered, "Give me the money so I can pay for it."

Not understanding, I loudly blurted out, "Why do you want me to give you the money to pay? I'm paying it."

He was upset, but I didn't think anything other than it was a strange thing for him to do.

Back in England, we talked about his plans for making a living. Having been educated to degree level and actively involved in local politics in Jamaica, I had made assumptions about his skill level and his financial situation.

Little by little, it became clear that his skill was farming, and he had no money whatsoever, which he was embarrassed about.

In fact, he was permanently distressed about not being able to assist his children and their mother who had financial difficulties where they lived in the USA. One of his daughters was also unwell. He asked me to help him with this.

By now, I thought he was using me and only wanted to marry me because I could help him with his financial difficulties, which he hadn't shared with me before and I didn't ask about.

This was yet another occasion when my emotional need for acceptance got in the way of logical thinking!

I decided to call his bluff and told him that, rather than send money to his children and their mother, let's try to get his sick daughter to live with us. I never heard anything more of this after that.

When it came to a job, he seemed reluctant to try, and I was impatient, threatening to throw him out unless he found work. Again, the mission to meet my need for acceptance prevented me from seeing who he was being. The same way I didn't see Fitz. I only saw what I wanted to see in my haste to meet my needs.

During this time, I realised that I knew very little about Trevor. I learned that he wasn't at all confident, not just because this was a strange country but because he had decided that it wasn't necessary to 'overexert' himself, as he saw it.

We were comfortably off, and he was happy cooking for us, staying at home and being the house husband that I did not want.

Six months into the marriage, the overwhelming positive feeling of being accepted by someone had worn off. I needed it, I got it, and, after that, I realised I had been searching for the wrong thing.

This, coupled with my irritation with my husband's attitude, resulted in my decision to end the marriage. He wasn't happy about it because I think by now he was beginning to believe we could make it through.

The end of the marriage was fairly straightforward. I outlined my reasons, and he eventually agreed that we were incompatible. Although it did not deliver on my expectations, this marriage was one of the best things to happen to me.

Without it, I don't think I'd have realised that the only form of acceptance that fulfilled me, was my acceptance of myself.

I had to get approval from someone else to see that I really needed to approve of myself. I was finally able to see that it isn't other people's acceptance that I needed to fill the hole left by my first and subsequent experiences of rejection.

I realised that I had to believe in myself and accept that I am perfect, whole and complete just the way I am.

After this experience, my life-long recurring dream of me falling down the gully and suddenly waking up to realise I was safe, stopped. I have never had it again. I know now that I have always had an inbuilt safety net that had never forsaken me. It has kept me alive.

# Clear Water

The struggle to heal the strained relationships with my family has been a life-long quest. I recently visited them in New York to attend my brother Tony's funeral. He passed away suddenly in his sleep.

While there, I went to a restaurant with my brother-in-law Clay, his wife and my niece. Over dinner, Clay told me that he and Loretta were very worried when I ran away those years ago. He said that they drove around Brooklyn looking for me. He wanted to tell me about their pain. I didn't want to have this conversation now. I wanted to scream,

*I existed! I exist now! Don't I get to have a choice about what we talk about? Don't you remember what life was like for me?*

*I wondered if I should tell him how her assault on me affected me? Couldn't he understand that I was often afraid to go home? Should I tell him that this was the reason why I needed to get away on those occasions?*

He clearly didn't know and couldn't see events through my eyes.

*Didn't he know that I have carried a belief that people think I am a thief ever since that first wrongful accusation by my great-aunt and then when I took the $5 notes?*

*now that this is the bewildering ghost still alive
'its? Didn't he know that I am embarrassed that
...ns and other things about me to his daughter and
wife, sitting with us at the table?*

Despite having the knowledge that it was not my fault, the stain still lingered within me even in adulthood. I could feel the lump of defeat in my throat. But I didn't express my thoughts.

"I went to the church at the end of the road," was all that I could utter.

He looked at me but didn't say any more. I don't think he believed me. So, I hastily attempted to change the subject and to divert the other's watchful eyes. I offered no other explanations because how could I tell him everything that happened when I am so ashamed of it? How could I get the words out of my mouth?

In recent times, I finally got to know about my mother, Rosita. As Loretta died some thirty years previously, I didn't get the chance to ask her any questions. If she had lived, I don't know if we might have reached the point where I felt confident enough to ask her any questions or attempt to mend our relationship. I hope we could have, armed with the understanding I now have of her and of myself that I didn't have as a child

However, supported by my wonderful son, I finally summoned up the courage to go and ask my older brother to tell me about my mother. Aged fifty-five, I went to Georgia to visit Roberto, whom I had not seen in many years. He told me that my mother and her siblings were born in Costa Rica. Her father left Jamaica to go there to work as a young man, a common occurrence as it was necessary for many men to leave the island to find work to survive.

My grandfather met his wife there. They had children and started to educate them before deciding to take them back to live in his country, Jamaica. Both of my mother's parents later died, we don't know how, leaving my mother, Rosita and her brothers to fend for themselves, in Jamaica.

According to my brother, our mother was a workaholic. He thought it was her industriousness that killed her. In Jamaica, she opened a small food shop in front of a cemetery, as it was on the main road where she could attract customers. She was required to gain permission from the local preacher to do so. She did this determined to ensure that her children were educated and fed.

During the day, she served lunch to school children of bulla, cheese, fry fish, bread and soda pop. At night, she sold fry fish and bread to late night revellers.

What Roberto said about our mother reminded me of the time I was in Jamaica on holiday while being driven by a local cab driver.

"You are Miss Rosita's baby, the last one," he declared.

I confirmed I was.

"I will never forget that woman," he smiled. "One day when I was at school, I went to her shop, and I had only enough money to buy a bulla cake. She looked at me for a little while then gave me a free lunch of fish, bread, soda everything."

At the end of the ride, he refused to take my money.

"It's the least I can do," he said.

Roberto said that our mother was always concerned for 'her girls' wanting to protect them and worrying about them. He explained that our mother had to bring up her children without the fathers because they needed to go abroad to work.

Rosita eventually went to America to join her brother Alfredo after he emigrated there. Soon after, she arranged for four of her children to follow, apart from the baby (me). She couldn't do that as it was cold in New York and she didn't know yet how to make a living. Besides, who would look after me while she was working? She considered it necessary to make life okay before I could join her.

In America, my mother first worked away from home, caring for old people in their own homes, leaving the older children looking after the younger ones with the help of our Uncle Alfredo. Roberto told me that Rosita became ill with cancer very early after her arrival in America.

I asked Roberto for a picture of our mother in America. He shared one of her standing outside the Brooklyn house, looking proud. I also got another of her when she graduated from her training as a nursing assistant.

"She worked too hard, she died too early!" Roberto sighed. "She was in her forties, it was too young."

He cried during his description of our mother's life, such was his love for this amazing woman. A woman about whom I only gained insight so many years after she left me at the tender age of two.

It was only in this conversation that I realised my mother had not meant me ill. On her deathbed in 1967, she asked Roberto to take care of 'her girls', including me. Again, I could feel and see the murky waters of my past clearing.

However, I believe her request for him to look after her girls was unreasonable, too much responsibility. I know this is not uncommon in some cultures, but this does not make it okay. The guilt he clearly feels about me and all that happened to me is an unfair burden for him to have carried all these years.

I was deeply affected by this conversation. I don't think Roberto knew how much this meant to me.

Someone with no hidden agenda was telling me about my mother. At last, I knew she didn't hate me. It was overwhelming.

It was all I could do to stay composed for the rest of the trip, so giddy was I with this momentous realisation.

When I got back to London, the hug I gave my son when he met me at the airport was like no other before. I clung to him and cried. It was a relief to come back home, more whole than ever before.

He was the only one who knew how much this trip meant to me. As he drove me home, I told him about the conversation with Roberto, and we both cried.

"Mom, I... am... so... proud of you," he choked.

"Thank you, darling, for every ounce of your support," I replied, shaking. "It helped so much knowing you had my back. That was the most difficult thing I have ever done. It wasn't easy to ask the question that I always dreaded the answer to."

As I spoke, I was crying tears of joy, not sadness. I finally achieved closure. Now I could breathe! I could see, the water that was my life was no longer murky, it was clear.

# EPILOGUE

*How I survived and thrive...*

# Epilogue

I had been busy being everyone's advisor, counsellor, manager and leader. For my part, I gained a lot of support from sharing my thoughts and feelings with my friends. This helped greatly but, after a difficult situation at work, I realised that I needed additional help.

I was running a child protection service when some extra work was dumped on me by my manager before she went on holiday. I reacted to this in an exaggerated way. The trigger was the disrespectful way she'd spoken to me. Indignant, I wrote her a letter detailing my reason for finding her behaviour unacceptable. I included everything she'd ever done that was not okay with me. The letter ended with my resignation.

Although initially pleased with myself for not tolerating her bad behaviour and poor delegation skills, I knew my response was disproportionate. It was after this that I sought out Christine, my counsellor.

During one of my sessions with Christine, I heard myself say, "What is it with these women in my life?" I meant my female manager, my great-aunt, my sister-mother.

Christine's work with me made it clear that I needed to unpack and understand my experiences. I wanted to start with my manager, but Christine helped me to begin with my mother, the person who first made decisions that she couldn't avoid but that left me feeling unworthy.

One day, in one of my sessions with Christine, I mentioned that I didn't like to look at myself, a fact that was pointed out to me when I had a session with a personal stylist.

Christine asked me to move to a bigger chair and imagine sitting next to my child self. She asked me what I'd say to Pam, the child. I couldn't even speak to her. I just cried. Little girl Pam needed a hug, she needed to be embraced by adult Pam. I don't remember what else happened just that I was overwhelmed. Recognising that I had locked her away was cathartic. This was difficult because I realised that I had put the child in me away, locked away because of how painful life was for her. Instead, I was existing as an adult pretending not to have my past and certainly not accepting it fully.

I realised then that I was only being a shell of myself, I was not an integrated person. No wonder people thought they could 'blow me over' with the strength of their words. The result of this ongoing work with Christine was that I became absolutely clear that there was nothing wrong with me. The people who had doled out the abuse were people with unmet needs, with serious problems and these people came from all walks of life, not only from my family, they were also in the workplace.

After that, with the help of some of my colleagues and my son, who listened and encouraged me, I realised that I had the understanding and knowledge of how to function despite actual or perceived obstacles. I was helped to see that I had a tremendous amount of strength, wisdom, and expertise.

It struck me more than ever, that my mission was to help people in similar situations as me. To enable them to understand the range of issues at play in their lives, both personal and professional, and how to handle them. This was the biggest teaching of all, which revolutionised my work.

It led me onto developing an experiential leadership and management training business which has been running for the last seven years. Our programmes have been influenced by what my experiences taught me about what people do and need. To design the programmes that we deliver, I go into organisations to gain an understanding of the challenges and to observe the culture, including how people relate to each other.

After that, I create specific bespoke programmes of training and development using my academic knowledge of leadership and management, my lived experience and my successes at leading people. I searched for highly effective group coaches who could help. Each person delivering the training believe people can learn and grow, bringing with them extensive knowledge of techniques and strategies to manage self and others. They are also able to use research from the world of neuroscience, Neuro-linguistic Programming (NLP) and behavioural psychology.

Trainers are required to convey an intention to teach and coach, egos have to be kept in check. Emotional intelligence is a pre-requisite. Delegates attending are asked to bring and share real-life problems and how they have handled them. This enables us to help them better manage themselves and situations.

All courses have workshops included and a 360-degree evaluation so that delegates can become aware of the perceptions others have of them, to understand what they might need to improve on. The accompanying individual coaching helps people to take responsibility for the experience they have at work, and in their lives.

Over the years, the courses have become better and better, and they are now delivered in a range of sectors; social work, health and large and small companies. Delegates tell me they are transformational. I also coach and mentor managers at all levels. Participants often say that I am courageous and that I helped them to find their own courage.

Nothing pleases me more than seeing people be all that they can be.

Over the years, I have continued to nurture myself to keep me connected to the fact that there is nothing wrong with me, and that I am good enough.

I have taken many courses in counselling, coaching, and self-help, retaining from them what makes sense to me and discarding what doesn't. These things helped but the most significant healing mechanism was the knowledge that my mother did not want to discard me.

Friends tell me that is what moved me to another level of self-confidence. As a result of all this, life is so much better for me now. I somehow communicate that I am no one's victim and my contribution to others is so much more impactful and speedy having broken the grip of most of my self-limiting beliefs.

Another friend recently told me that in the thirty years he has known me, I have been determined to find myself.

"Yes," I declared. "I have been looking for the fully optimised me."

I am closer now than I have ever been. Surprisingly, the freedom I feel now after writing this book is like none that I have felt before. I realise that writing is an important therapeutic tool, although it certainly isn't easy.

There were many occasions when I wanted to stop. Times when I felt it took too much to relive the experiences in order to write about them. I also wondered whether I was sharing too much. Every time I had these thoughts someone, either my son, my niece, my friend or a conversation at work led me back to the thought it might help someone. The compulsion to help and to have my pain and learning prompt others to use theirs was impossible to resist. My experiences have afforded me a level of insight into human behaviour that I wouldn't have without them. For that I am thankful.

*Back in Jamaica, some fifty years after I planted them, the mango trees are still there in the yard. They are bent double from the Caribbean climate, living on through the storms and the sun, grateful for the rain when it comes. The trees, like me, have survived.*

# About the Author
# Pam Rowe

Pam has been a social worker for over thirty years'. Working in local and central government, she also led, inspected, established, reviewed and project-managed improvements in Children's Services. Her roles have included Assistant Director and Deputy Director.

Pam is honoured to be a leader of services to children using her experience to transform the relationship that, social workers, leaders, children and families have with themselves.

Since 2011, she has been running her own business evaluating how organisations function before delivering transformational leadership training programmes. Her company also provides coaching to individuals' who all say they have transformed their lives as a result.

She believes that dealing with ourselves and shifting our self-limiting beliefs, focusing on the cause, not just the symptoms, is the key to contributing in a positive way to humanity.

Her experiences have taught her that it is only by owning and being honest about our past and its impact on us, can we move beyond it and fulfil our function in the world.

# Addendum

# Reflections

With my experiences, I could not have chosen any other profession, other than that of helping children and adults who are just normal people whose childhood experiences are still affecting them.

Without what I have been through my 'line of sight' could not have been achieved. My first-hand experience of abuse is why I understand the impact of abuse on the ability of people to function as adults. My life has given me insight into what people need to do and how they need to be to counteract the manifestation of the impact of all types of abuse. This is why I am effective in helping people to be empowered and to change.

One fundamental fact that I have gleaned from my life of learning, the most significant point for adults and parents to remember is that, you yourself were once a child.

Consider what you needed then and what you know with hindsight. It is no different for your children. They need to know and understand life just as you did.

In communicating with your children and others' children give answers to the questions you asked when you were a child.

Parents and carers, please give your children positive childhood memories by telling them good things about themselves from as early in life as possible. Ensure that they experience positive connections, both physical and emotional and repeat it, repeat it, repeat it.

I received some of this positive reinforcement from my Aunt Dar when I was very young, in Jamaica. Ever since then, it has been the basis for my resilience. With everything that happened, I always remembered that I was loved by my Uncle John and that Aunt Dar said I was smart and quick enough to be anything I wanted to be.

Hold on to your children, you are responsible for them. It's your job to protect them. Every child needs someone who can see when they are in need of positivity. It was devastating that the economic situation in Jamaica, meant that my mother could not 'hold on' to me.

In my life, the emotional positives came from my social worker, the teachers, and my cousin who sat and talked to me and even my uncle who said, "Never mind," when I needed to hear that. They were so important that I still remember them today.

From the start, build the type of close, healthy relationship with your child that will enable them to tell you what is happening in their lives. Stay close to them as they grow up. Talk a lot to them. Anticipate what could happen and help direct their lives, but also listen to them. Remember, listening to children is not the same as always doing what they say. What they say is information for you to take into account when you make decisions.

Ensure children have a hobby, a sport, an interest and support them in doing it. Help them build good relationships with others. Many people can play a part in helping you, it takes a village to bring up a child.

Always ensure good communication. It is vital to speak with children directly about important issues regarding their lives, including decisions and events.

I appreciate that you may not know about particular techniques to use, but words will do. How the words are spoken will reflect your thoughts and feelings and how they are received. Take the time to think about this and then start talking to your children.

Violence as a response to behaviours is not acceptable. When Aunt Dar assaulted me, how did it help? When my sister Loretta attacked me, what did she think she was changing? The only thing they achieved was to impart fear in me and a deep sense of foreboding, which has taken a lifetime for me to overcome. How confusing and contradictory for a caregiver to also inflict physical pain upon a child.

Beatings have a huge impact on the sense of safety and security of any child.

Some may ask, "What's the big deal?"

It is not right to hit a child, under any circumstances, is my reply.

What are we doing when we respond in this way and mete out extreme violence upon a child? When we do this, what is the difference between the slaves and their masters and parents and their children?

If we agree that the beating of slaves is wrong, then the beating or hitting of our children and the children we care for is also wrong.

We must stop the violent assault on children and young people, it does not build our communities, our families, or our children. It simply breaks them down.

A frightened child becomes an adult who has an additional barrier or deficit to overcome in terms of their confidence and belief in their own-selves. Is that what we want? Our own negative experiences do not have to continue to be inflicted upon future generations. The old adage, "I got hit and it did me no harm," is not true. We may not appreciate the harm it did but believe me, it did harm, and until we acknowledge it, there can be no hope that this can change.

Using phrases such as "I'm going to teach you a lesson!" as part of a physical assault on a child serves no purpose. All I gained from these 'lessons' was a sense of powerlessness, unfairness and defeat.

These injustices can fester and turn into anger and violence which can be meted out to others when we are children and later as adults. Some, who were beaten, assault their wives, husbands and children later on. Some take drugs or get lost in an alcoholic stupor or suffer with psychological and emotional health issues. Is this what we want to give to our children? Is this the legacy we want to pass on?

Try to take a step back and understand behaviours. Take a moment to consider what might be going on for a child. There is always a reason for a child's behaviour, however inconvenient it might be. Stop for a minute to ask what could be going on for a child or adult with challenging behaviours. This way we may stand a chance of stopping violence by adults against children. A label of 'bad child' or 'bad person' will not change it. Describing behaviour and attaching judgement upon children is not helping at all.

When Aunt Dar labelled me a thief, it did not help me. It wasn't true, but the impact was lasting. I thought that everyone else believed it and it affected what I felt about other people.

For many years it made me self-conscious when I went back to Jamaica. When my sister focused on me taking her money, she was focusing on a behaviour. She did not recognise that it was a call for help. I was powerless to affect the thinking of the adults around me, I had to keep guessing and imagining. This gave me an additional worry when I should have been free to just be me.

Behaviours are symptoms of deeper problems. Sometimes you must imagine what the fundamental problem could be. Consider, what would it be for you if you were the child?

Forming an open relationship with direct lines of communication with any young person will always help.

After I was gang-raped, my sister Loretta aggressively berated me. I know that when something catastrophic happens, it is hard to be balanced and not hit out at the person or child, who you blame. But, parents and adults, before you unleash your wrath, please speak to someone, a friend, a professional, a family member, a counsellor or therapist.

For a child or young person who has experienced trauma, it does not help when you attack them. It makes it worse. Can you imagine being in shock, ashamed and feeling responsible, only to be met with words and actions that confirm that you are to blame?

It is not helpful to ask the child why they behaved problematically and in a challenging way. Which is what Loretta did with me when she asked, why I took the money or why I ran away. I have often wondered why adults, parents and professionals believe that a child has the ability to analyse their own behaviours rationally.

Are we really asking children and young people to say, "Well, the emotional trauma, separation, loss and other issues that I have experienced is the trigger for my current behaviour. What will really help me is if you did this or that!" Are we asking them to answer us like this? Many adults cannot explain and analyse their own behaviour, therefore, is it reasonable to expect a child to be able to do this?

In the incident with my sister-mother, I could only say, "I took the money." I could not give a reason. I could not explain why. I didn't say, "Well I wanted to be accepted, I wanted to be like other children." How could I, when I didn't realise this was the reason at the time?

I also did not understand that it was her wedding money that Loretta had worked hard to secure. No one told me or involved me in the dynamics of the household. It is only now as an adult that I can see what the money meant to her. Why should she have to tell me anything? Because I am a person, I exist. I was not a cardboard cut-out devoid of feelings, thoughts or the ability to understand. Children are people, small ones, but people nonetheless.

My story also brings up important issues about children co-parenting. When I think about Loretta's life, I realise that as the older girl, she spent her life co-parenting, resenting it and taking out her anger about it on me. To her, it must have seemed that she was born to be a parent from the start.

So, parents, please think about the pressure you put your older children under when you give them the responsibility of caring for your younger children.

It is not fair. They don't have the freedom to be themselves. They are co-parents from the beginning of their lives. It is perfectly understandable if they later become controlling, resentful and even bitter.

Your children are your responsibility and no-one else's. The UK's focus on supporting young carers and giving them respite is right. Young carers also include siblings who parent their brothers and sisters. Think about what these children need and do not hesitate to help them.

Also, if a child or adult is new to a country, try to put yourself in their shoes. Do not assume that they understand everything. Consider that you may have to explain simple things which you often take for granted. When I arrived in New York, from rural Jamaica, I found it bewildering but no one thought they should explain anything to me. Therefore, I naively wandered into dangerous situations.

To help prevent child sexual abuse and exploitation, tell children what forms of behaviours are appropriate, from adults, other children and young people. Tell them how to protect themselves and who is around to protect them. My father's sexual abuse of me took me by surprise. I didn't expect that the person who I thought came to my rescue after years of ill-treatment and trauma, was to be the person who abused me and took advantage of my vulnerability. I didn't know who to tell. I didn't know about any services that could help.

We have national campaigns about drink driving or road safety. Why are there not more effective national and international campaigns raising awareness for parents about the dangers of abusing or harming their children? To prevent child sexual abuse and exploitation, children and adults need to be taught what kinds of behaviours are and aren't appropriate. Encourage children to tell someone. Abusers rely on silence to mask their deeds. If they can instil fear in their prey, they will.

Let's launch a 'Speak Out' campaign. Even if children don't feel they can speak out, the fact that we are encouraging them might cause a few abusers to be cautious or better still to be afraid to abuse children. Adult survivors of abuse must be supported to speak about their experiences in childhood.

We must do more to enlist businesses, entrepreneurs, and people in the community to be interested and active in what is going on for children and young people, with a view to protecting them.

The media, internet and broadcasting sector must be utilised to help raise awareness globally, as they do with other issues. Life-threatening issues like Ebola can galvanise nations, why can't potentially fatal emotional events like child abuse get the same kind of attention?

It is not beyond us to make a difference. Are we afraid of the costs of reporting individual cases? Prevention campaigns could save money and more importantly save lives! Why is this so often left to a charity or to whomever, after one appalling incident follows another? It is cost effective to invest in awareness raising and prevention to have the population aware and safe. It is cost effective to focus on the cause not just the symptom of people's behavior.

Fathers and mothers get help to curb your violence, or sexual inappropriateness, your perversions and desires for sexual relations with children and family members.

Get help if you live with the fact that you were sexually abused.

Partners, mothers, fathers and step-mothers, I understand that when your relationship is fragile, you don't want to lose the man or woman who is meeting your needs. You may not want to risk acting or speaking out against a behaviour or perversion. Please think about this again. Children and young people need you. Sometimes you are their only hope, the only possibility of the abuse stopping. Get help with your feelings. Tell someone about your dilemma. Ask for help. Find organisations that specialise in these issues.

Governments, please make support available to parents who collude with the abuse their partners mete out. It seems the only approach we have to this group of people is to punish them when they have colluded with extreme abuse.

Teachers, please understand how important you are to children. For some children, school is the only positive environment where there is any sense of reward and gratification that isn't affected by abuse. Schools and education had an essential role in my life, it was where I picked up the message that there was nothing wrong with me.

Schools, please continue to equip children with the self-esteem and self-belief they need. This will help to build a barrier against abuse.

It will help those children who need it, to remove the 'cloak of victim' the evident vulnerability that perpetrators can spot. You can and do help when you engender confidence in your students, when you reward their success and help them when they are struggling.

You don't have to be an abuse specialist, to raise awareness about how children can learn to protect themselves.

By creating a general atmosphere of openness, safety and trust, the difference you make can be incredible. You know this already.

You do not just make an academic difference, you make a fundamental difference to the functioning of children and then adults in society.

Make yourself aware of and then tell children about the dangers that exist, for example, what to do when there is 'stranger danger' or what to do if a family member is sexually abusing them.

Let us not operate as though we are not human beings who are not affected by events. The manifestation of traumatic experiences will materialise, at some point.

I know we have to keep going. We may think that to talk about emotions is a luxury. It is not, it is an absolute necessity and it is vital if we are not to cause damage to our children, our siblings, others and ourselves. Get help with how you feel about your life. Whoever you are in society, you need someone, people who can stop you from holding onto anger and prevent it from leaking out.

Get help to support yourself, to stop you taking it out on the most vulnerable, your children or people who you think are not like you, and who you imagine are less than you.

Talk to your friends, a counsellor, or a coach about how you feel. Stop yourself taking it out on others.

The damage you do is lasting. The help they will need to recover will be extensive.

Parents, if you have abused your children and feel guilt and shame, firstly acknowledge it, then forgive yourself and never do it again. Secondly when the adult child asks you about what happened please don't deny it. Get help to assist you with healing and forgiveness.

If we are to be healthy adults, contributing to others in the most impactful ways, don't we need to look after our children well? My own experiences taught me that the damage done in childhood can be lasting. Look how long it took me to accept that there was nothing wrong with me, to accept myself. I had to learn from the choices I made about the impact my childhood experiences had on my adult relationships.

I hope these thoughts will help a child, a parent, or any human being in need. If sharing my experiences can help others, then everything I have been through has been worthwhile.

# Clear Water

## Pam Rowe

## Reviews of Clear Water by Pam Rowe

"As I read about Pam's experiences from her early childhood through to maturity, I was humbled by her endurance and determination to survive in spite of the emotional and physical pain inflicted on her. There are so many lessons to be learnt from Pam's book about how to care for and about children and adults. For me, the overriding lesson is the need for each of us to take responsibility for understanding ourselves in order to understand each other better."

**Mary Walker** – Mother and Grandmother

"This is not a sad 'tea and sympathy' memoir but rather a story of 'overcoming'. *Clear Water* reminds the reader that human beings need compassion and children need the parents and caregivers in their lives to be compassionate."

**Sandra Miller** – Social Worker, Editorial Reviewer.

"Clear Water is a story that we can all relate to. I was able to have a different perspective on situations that have not happened to me and relate to those that did with clarity. There were quite a few 'aha' moments when the cloudy water of my own understanding became very clear."

**Audrey Jackson** - Widow and Mother

To find out more about Pam Rowe go to her website

www.pamrowe.com

Printed in Great Britain
by Amazon